# The Struts Framework

## Practical Guide for Java Programmers

**The Morgan Kaufmann Practical Guides Series**
Series Editor: Michael J. Donahoo

*The Struts Framework: Practical Guide for Java Programmers*
Sue Spielman

*Java: Practical Guide for Programmers*
Zbigniew M. Sikora

*Multicast Sockets: Practical Guide for Programmers*
David Makofske and Kevin Almeroth

*TCP/IP Sockets in Java: Practical Guide for Programmers*
Kenneth L. Calvert and Michael J. Donahoo

*TCP/IP Sockets in C: Practical Guide for Programmers*
Michael J. Donahoo and Kenneth L. Calvert

*JDBC: Practical Guide for Java Programmers*
Gregory D. Speegle

For further information on these books and for a list of forthcoming titles, please visit our Web site at *www.mkp.com/practical*.

# The Struts Framework

## Practical Guide for Java Programmers

**Sue Spielman**

Switchback Software LLC

MORGAN KAUFMANN PUBLISHERS

AN IMPRINT OF ELSEVIER SCIENCE

AMSTERDAM BOSTON LONDON NEW YORK
OXFORD PARIS SAN DIEGO SAN FRANCISCO
SINGAPORE SYDNEY TOKYO

*Senior Editor* Rick Adams
*Publishing Services Manager* Edward Wade
*Senior Production Editor* Cheri Palmer
*Developmental Editor* Karyn Johnson
*Cover Design* Yvo Riezebos
*Cover Image* © Sherman/Getty Images
*Text Design* Side by Side Studios/Mark Ong
*Composition and Illustration* Windfall Software, using ZzTeX
*Copyeditor* Robert Fiske
*Proofreader* Carol Leyba
*Indexer* Steve Rath
*Printer* The Maple-Vail Book Manufacturing Group



Morgan Kaufmann Publishers
An imprint of Elsevier Science
340 Pine Street, Sixth Floor
San Francisco, CA 94104-3205
*www.mkp.com*


Printed in the United States of America

07 06 05 04 03 5 4 3



**Library of Congress Control Number: 2002108513**
ISBN: 1-55860-862-1

This book is printed on acid-free paper.

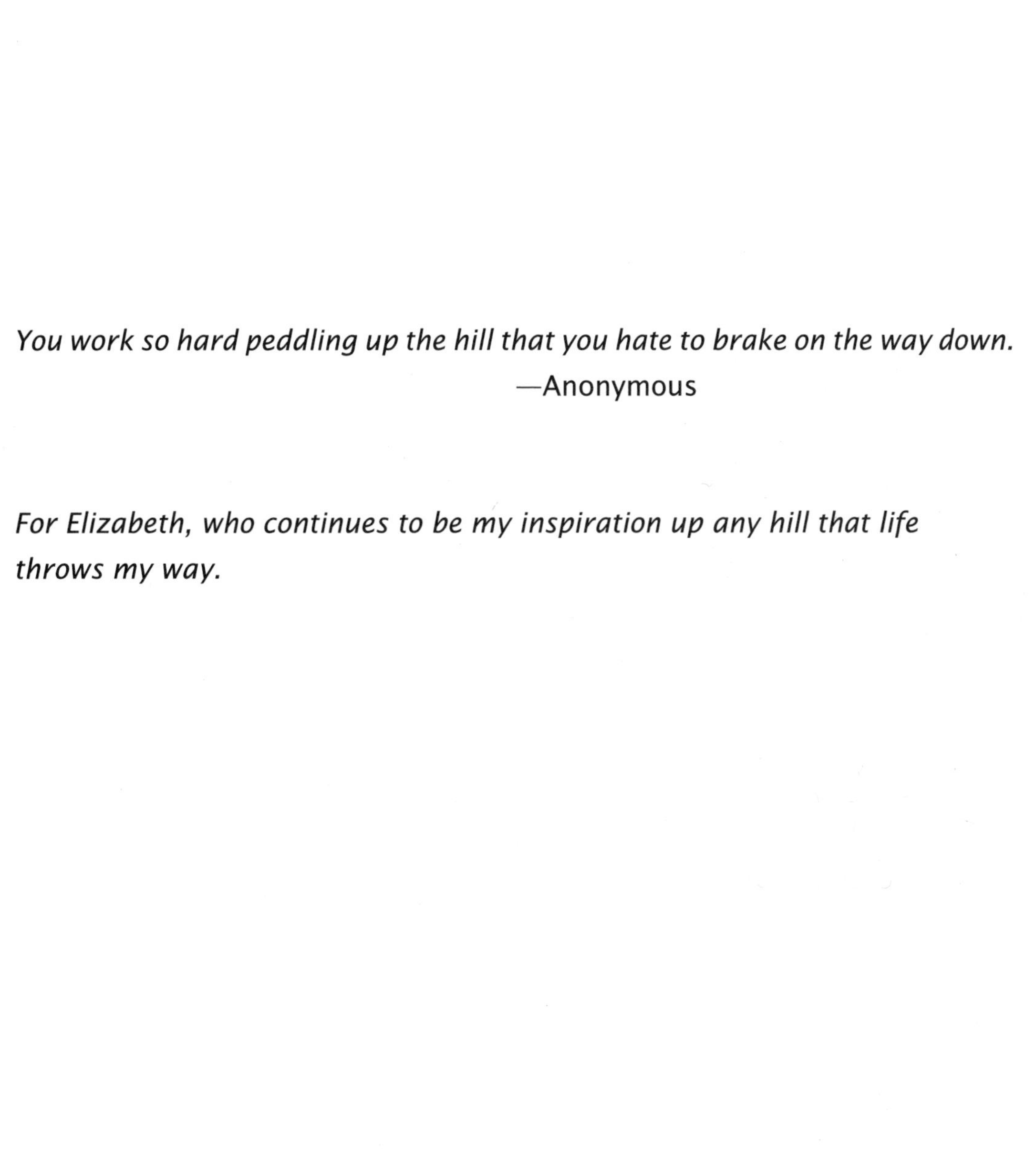

*You work so hard peddling up the hill that you hate to brake on the way down.*

—Anonymous

*For Elizabeth, who continues to be my inspiration up any hill that life throws my way.*

# Contents

# Preface

Keeping up with the latest and greatest innovations in the high-tech industry is a job unto itself. My purpose in writing this book is to help you come up to speed as quickly as possible with using the Struts 1.1 framework. “Come up to speed” in this context means understanding the architecture and the technologies involved, as well as understanding how to start building applications. In order to accomplish all this, I need to make some basic assumptions about you. Normally, I don’t like making assumptions about people, but in this case it’s required. Maybe it’s better to tell you what I’m expecting from you so that you can judge for yourself whether or not you’re going to be challenged in some areas. You should know though that I’ll give you pointers to where you can get more information on a topic that might be beyond the very specific focus of this book. The pointers are provided both in the text of the book and in Appendix B so that you can reference them by topic.

This is a book about the Struts 1.1 framework, and the word *framework* is important. Struts is not a specific technology; rather, it’s made up of a number of technologies. This makes it more challenging for me to ensure that you understand the overall concepts of Struts as well as its underlying technology. Therefore, I also must tell you what this book isn’t. This is not a book to learn the fundamentals of Object-Oriented programming; it is also not a book to learn Java. OO concepts and the Java programming language are used extensively throughout this book. So I am assuming that you have a solid understanding of both and that you have programmed in Java before.

The most helpful technology for you to have under your belt is JavaServer Pages. If you’ve written some Servlets and Java web applications, that’s great, but this book is really for those who are now anxious to hone their skills specific to Struts. Along the way, you will learn some of the workings of other J2EE technologies. There are experienced programmers, newcomers to software, and aspiring students out there. You’ll each be faced with the challenge of finding your way through the hype and the theory to arrive at something concrete that explains, very simply, how to go about thinking, designing, and developing a web based project using Java and Struts. This book will help get you there.

## Author Approach

This book follows the 80/20 rule. You will find between its covers the information to get you started using Struts and that helps you accomplish 80% of what you'll need to do in application development.

So what about the other 20%? When developing applications, it's usually that 20% that takes the most time. This includes using the most advanced features to solve the most difficult problems. While I'll give you pointers and solutions to some areas that might be in that 20%, for the most part this book is going to give you the 80% and I'll save the balance for the sequel. I'm not saying I'll avoid some of the more complicated (or confusing) issues. It's just that if you find something has been left out, it is likely because my development experience said it was a feature that fell into that 20% range.

While JSP and Servlet technology have been around for a number of years now, the evolution of the models used has grown as more complex applications were developed. This has been a constant challenge for developers because as applications grow, so do the complexities. This book demonstrates ways that development can be simplified even if the development requirements grow continually more complex. That is also the beauty of Struts: Struts solves more complicated problems quickly and keeps them manageable.

In order to take you through as many of the Struts features as possible, and since I'm actually a developer, and don't just play one on TV, I decided to take a development style approach to this book. The book uses a sample application that we will define and build throughout. Instead of using random code snippets, most (if not all) of the code samples and snippets that you will find are part of the sample download application. You can view, examine, and explore all the code in the context that it lives in, not just in the two or three lines I might use to explain or demonstrate a point. I believe this practical approach leaves you with a more thorough understanding of not only the concepts, but also how to apply them.

## Sample Application

The sample application used throughout this book can be downloaded in all its glory detail, or gory detail, whichever you prefer. Whether this is your first application or not, you'll find that you can use all or only parts of this application as a starting point for your own development projects. It is built using the JDK 1.3.1 running on Tomcat 4.0.1. While it's not mandatory that you download and run the application as you progress through the book, I think you will find it incredibly helpful to do so.

Many of the available features in the Struts 1.1 release are used in this book. The sample application uses the Apache ANT 1.4.1 build tool as the build environment. I've provided a full and complete `build.xml` file with multiple targets at *www.mkp.com/practical/struts*. It is possible to build, and rebuild, from all the source files provided. I've scaled the `build.xml` down from real production applications I've built, but it serves well for starting your own application development script. If you need more details on ANT you can find it at *jakarta.apache.org/ant/index.html*.

For those not familiar with Tomcat, it is the reference implementation of the JSP/Servlet specification and can be used as a JSP container. It is open source and it's free. You can download it from *jakarta.apache.org/tomcat/index.html.* Follow the install instructions available on the Tomcat site. It should not take more than 10 minutes to download and install.

I've also tried to make this as close to a real application as possible without introducing some of the more complex issues associated with development. In a real application, you typically use Enterprise JavaBeans (EJB) to implement your business logic as well as a robust database. I've decided to avoid using EJBs in this book because they're beyond the scope. I've hooked up a sample database using MySQL (open source and free and available at *www.mysql.com*), and have included a database script so that you can download the database, follow the install directions off the site, and run the database install script called `CdManagerDB.txt`, which I've provided at the book's web site. This script creates the necessary table and populates it with data so that you will be ready to hit the road running. Doing these steps will also allow you to get more familiar with the actual setup and environment that you would probably be running an application in.

## Acknowledgments

An acknowledgments section is one of the few times that one gets to give an Oscar acceptance like speech, so here goes. As with anything that requires much time, effort, and coffee, there are always others behind the scenes who make a huge contribution to the final product.

I'd like to thank Jeff Donahoo at Baylor University for coming across my articles posted on OnJava.com and liking them enough to ask me to write this book. Thanks to Karyn Johnson and Rick Adams at Morgan Kaufmann for providing their editorial expertise. Karyn, I'm still working on the Micheal Stipe picture. My gratitude to the technical reviewers: David McClure, Simon Chappell, Bob Lee, Tom Marrs, Tod Nguyen, and Gradin Hammell all gave excellent feedback and helped make this book better than it would have been without their input. Also, thanks to the initial proposal reviewers who include David McClure, James Couball, John Raley, Christopher Neubert, Ken Hoying, and Gregor Rayman.

Special thanks to Liz Winfeld for her outstanding job in making my technical jargon read correctly in English, which technically is my second language after Java. Muchas gracias and merci beaucoup to Kathy Evan and Toni Bogdon for lending their international language skills to the download sample application. Thanks to Bill Lowe for understanding all the times I missed cycling because I had "just one more" section I needed to finish. I would also like to thank the many developers and committers (too numerous to list here) who contribute to the Struts project. You should all give yourself a pat on the back for the fantastic job you do in bringing this project to life. Thanks to Craig McClanahan for taking the time out of his busy schedule to read this book and more important for turning his brain child into the Struts project.

Last, and what would any Oscar speech be without this, I'd like to thank my parents for, among other things, telling me to go into computers when I was in high school.

## Let's Get Going

Open source development in general is a moving target. I've used Struts 1.1 for the contents of this book, but chances are that there will be more features and newer releases to be had while this book is in print. Fear not, your money is still well spent. I will keep updates, comments, and corrections (if necessary) available on the Morgan Kaufmann web site at *www.mkp.com/practical/struts*.

So whether you are a new developer, an experienced developer, or a technical manager trying to figure out if Struts is for you, I hope that this book will bring Struts to life. Feel free to contact me at my email address and let me know if you have comments or suggestions about content, or just to let me know if the book helped you. I also suggest that if you are going to be working with Struts, sign up for the very active Struts-Users mailing list. In fact, I highly recommend signing up for the digest version by sending a request to struts-user-digest-subscribe@jakarta.apache.org . This will prevent you from being overwhelmed with the amount of email you'll get your very first day on the list. You can find the various resources for the mailing list at *jakarta.apache.org/struts/resources.html#archives.* This is really the best way to keep up with the current happenings with the project. All that said, let's go have some fun with Struts.

Sue Spielman
President/Senior Consulting Engineer
Switchback Software LLC
*www.switchbacksoftware.com*
sspielman@switchbacksoftware.com

chapter 1

# Struts and Enterprise Web Technologies

Struts is a Java-based framework used to build web applications. It's not a technology unto itself. We start off by making sure that everyone is on equal footing in terms of the technologies that we will be using. While this chapter is not code intensive, it is critical to engender an understanding of how all the technologies involved are used and what their purpose is.

## 1.1 Technology Stew

It is fairly common in today's development environment to be working with many interrelated technologies. Often it is necessary to have a thorough understanding of quite a few technologies to get a job done. Sometimes just keeping up with the various specifications and the latest happenings can be a monumental task.

The core Struts technologies are JavaServer Pages and Servlets. However, there are a few other areas that are helpful to be up on, including

- Custom tags
- XML
- Web and application servers

I'm not going to go into the details of all these technologies, but I wanted to set the stage with a brief description of each. Chances are that you will become involved with using these technologies during the course of your development. If you feel that you need more information, refer to the links provided to help you along. Figure 1.1 provides a glimpse of how each of the technologies we are interested in fits into the big picture of web application development. We will be talking about each of the components in detail throughout the book.

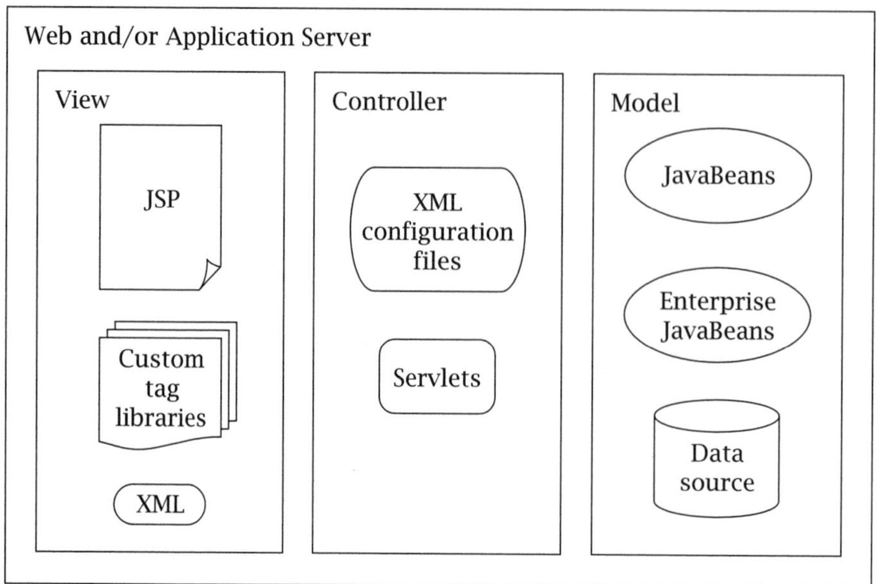


**Figure 1.1:** Technology overview.

### 1.1.1 JavaServer Pages

JavaServer Pages (JSP) is a technology used for building web applications that serve dynamic content. The JSP is a server-side component that is made up of static HTML or XML components, tags that are specific to JSP, and optional snippets of Java code called scriptlets. JSP is used as the presentation layer in n-tier web architectures to separate presentation from content. In the Struts framework, JSPs represent the View in the Model-View-Controller design pattern we talk about in Section 1.2. The JSP specification is an extension of the Servlet API, so it uses and leverages the Servlet context. JSPs allow for defining objects within certain scopes. The available scopes are page, request, session, and application. Figure 1.2 shows the availability of an object given a particular scope. Objects are visible to their ring or any inner rings, but not to outer rings of their defined scope.

Scope comes into play when dealing with objects such as JavaBeans, also just called Beans. The component model for JSP technology is based on JavaBeans component architecture. JavaBeans components are nothing but Java objects that follow a well-defined design/naming pattern using public accessor methods for reading and mutator methods for modifying the Beans property values. These are also called the familiar getter/setter methods spoken so much about. We'll see as we progress through the book how the Struts `ActionForm` class is actually nothing more than a Bean. The JavaBean specification can be found at *java.sun.com/products/javabeans/*.

Before you can access a Bean within a JSP page, you must identify and obtain a reference to it. The `<jsp:useBean>` tag tries to obtain a reference to an instance that already exists. It

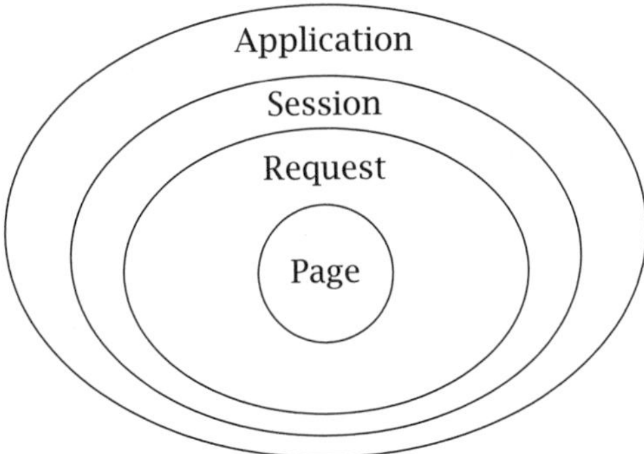


**Figure 1.2:** JSP object scopes.

does so by using the specified ID and scope. If the Bean was created previously and placed in a specific scope from another JSP, that instance will be used. If an instance isn't found, then a new instance is created. A sample JSP tag to do so might look like

```
<jsp:useBean id="user" class="cdmanager.user" scope="session" />
```

Struts makes use of Beans within its framework, so it's important to at least be familiar with the terminology.

When a JSP is first requested from an incoming request, it is parsed into a Java source file and then compiled into a Servlet class.

If you need more background on JSP development, see *java.sun.com/products/jsp/* or *java.sun.com/products/jsp/docs.html* for a tutorial.

### 1.1.2 Servlets

Servlets play a large role in web application development. Servlets are a Java technology-based solution that run inside a Java Virtual Machine (JVM). Since a Servlet runs in a JVM, it is a very portable technology. Servlets are generic server extensions that can be dynamically loaded when needed by the web server. The common request/response paradigm that we are all familiar with in regard to HTTP applies also to Servlets. The Java Servlet API is based on several Java interfaces that are provided in standard Java extension (`javax`) packages. The APIs are included in the `servlet.jar` file. The Servlet technology is mentioned because the controller in the Struts architecture is a Servlet. Technically, since all JSPs compile into Servlets anyway, it doesn't hurt to understand them.

For further Servlet information, refer to *java.sun.com/products/servlet/index.html* or *www.servlets.com.*

### 1.1.3 Custom Tag Libraries

JSP is the technology that strives to keep the frontend presentation separate from the middle and backend tiers. Custom tag libraries are a powerful feature available since JSP v1.1 that advance the march to that mantra. Custom tag libraries allow the Java programmer to write code that provides data access and other services, and they make those features available to the JSP author in a simple-to-use XML-like fashion. The JSP author does not have to understand any of the underlying details to complete the Action. In short, a tag library is nothing more than a collection of custom Actions presented as tags.

Struts has five powerful custom tag libraries that are used for building interactive, form-based web applications. There's a very detailed chapter coming up about how to use them in your development. If you need more information on custom tags, start with *java.sun.com/products/jsp/tutorial/TagLibrariesTOC.html* or *jsptags.com.*

## 1.1.4 XML

The eXtensible Markup Language (XML) is becoming, or more accurately has become, ubiquitous in web application and web services development. It is difficult to build an application these days without having to deal with XML. XML is used to represent structured documents and data on the web. It consists of a set of well-formed elements. Elements are well formed if they have both opening and closing tags and are nested properly within each other. For example,

```
<cd>
        <artist>Madonna</artist>
        <title>Ray of Light</title>
</cd>
```

represents three XML tags, cd, artist, and title. It's possible to validate XML files against a document type declaration (DTD). The XML DTD contains or points to markup declarations that provide a grammar for a class of documents. XML files are commonly used as configuration files for various applications, and Struts is no exception. The two XML files of interest to us in the Struts framework are `web.xml`, which is used for the web application configuration, and `struts-config.xml`, which is used for configuring all the actions that can be taken by your Struts application. A subsequent chapter will look at the configuration file setups.

For more information on XML, start with *www.w3.org/TR/2000/REC-xml-20001006* or *www.w3schools.com/xml/default.asp.*

## 1.1.5 Web and Application Servers

Web and application servers play a role in any web application. A web server handles the HTTP processing while an application server handles other services. These can be container services, such as a JSP container, or a complex handling of other web-related services such as Enterprise JavaBean (EJB) support, or they can be transaction support. Whether you will need to use a full-blown application server depends on how complicated your web application is. If you are using EJBs in your development, then you need an application server that can act as an EJB container. JBoss (*www.jboss.org*) is a freely available, industrial strength EJB container that comes bundled with Tomcat. If you are a developer who wants to use EJBs from the Action classes and needs to evaluate EJB containers, JBoss is worth a look.

Tomcat, which is what we will be using for our development, can be run as a web server as well as a JSP container. Tomcat is the source code basis for the official reference implementation of the JSP/Servlet specification. The files of interest to us are the configuration files used by the web server for our application. When using Tomcat, all web applications are placed under the `webapps` directory. It is possible to just place a web archive file (WAR file) into the `webapps` directory. When Tomcat starts, it checks for any new WAR files and automatically deploys them. There is a standard directory structure that is used for WAR files (which we'll discuss when we go into how to deploy your application) so that the server knows what to look for to deploy the application correctly.

The `web.xml` file is a configuration file that is used to specify Servlets to load for a web application. Struts makes use of the `web.xml` file. Struts applications can be run in any JSP 1.1 and Servlet 2.2 compliant container. There are differences in configurations for application servers, so if you are going to be using an application server other than Tomcat, you must make sure that you check its documentation for information about deploying web applications. There is a growing list of configuration instructions for various servers available on the Struts site's installation page link.

Another thing to note, as was mentioned earlier, is that when a JSP is accessed, it is compiled into a Servlet. When using Tomcat, the compiled Servlets are placed in a `work` subdirectory. In the `work` directory, you will probably see a `localhost` directory and then a number of subdirectories for each web application that you have on your server. The application we'll be working with will be in a `cdManagerSample` subdirectory.

When debugging, it is always helpful to delete the `work` directory and let Tomcat create it from scratch. That way you can be assured that you aren't working with an older compiled version of a file by accident. I've provided a deploy target in the build file for our application that will automatically delete the `work` directory so that you are always starting with a clean slate.

For more information on Tomcat, refer to *jakarta.apache.org/tomcat/index.html.*

## 1.2 Model-View-Controller

The Struts framework is very design pattern-oriented. This is good news for many developers since working with patterns usually makes life a little easier. Not only do patterns provide clean, proven designs, they also help the developer's learning curve. Once you are familiar with the pattern, it is easy to apply its concepts to various projects. The entire Struts framework is based on the Model-View-Controller (MVC) pattern. Sometimes you might also hear this referred to as the Model 2 approach, or MVC2, but we'll call it MVC.

The MVC pattern is a way of taking an application and breaking it into three distinct parts: the model, the view, and the controller. The pattern itself was originally developed to work in the graphical user interface (GUI) space, but it is successfully used in many—actually most—web applications. The advantage of using the MVC pattern is that there is no business or Model-specific processing within the presentation, or view, component itself. The opposite is

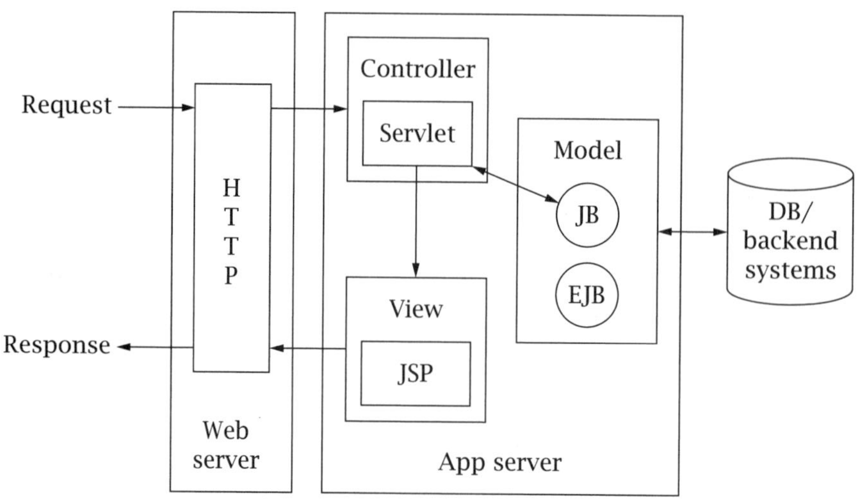


**Figure 1.3:** MVC pattern overview.

also true; that is, there is no presentation logic in the model and business layers. This improves component reuse there and also improves the ability to change a layer's implementations with minimal effect on the other layers. This is a key point and one of the main benefits of Struts. Let's take a look at each component, what its responsibility is, and how it correlates to the Struts components.

An overview of the MVC pattern's components is shown in Figure 1.3.

An important note to be made for the aspiring (or active) architects reading this book: if you design your MVC model components correctly, non-web clients can reuse the Model quite easily. If you need more information about how to specifically do this, look at the J2EE blueprints site located at *java.sun.com/blueprints/enterprise/index.html*. It will provide you with a good patterns-oriented approach.

### 1.2.1 General Flow

In the MVC design pattern, the application flow is mediated by a central Controller. The Controller delegates requests—in our case, HTTP requests—to an appropriate handler. A handler is nothing more than the set of logic that is used to process the request. In the Struts framework, the handlers are also called actions. The handlers are tied to a Model, and each handler acts as an adapter, or bridge, between the request and the Model. A handler or action typically uses one or more JavaBeans or EJBs to perform the actual business logic. The Action gets any information out of the request necessary to perform the desired business logic and then passes it along to the JavaBean or EJB.

The Model represents, or encapsulates, an application's business logic or state. Control is then usually forwarded back through the Controller. The Controller then dispatches to the appropriate View. The forwarding can be determined by consulting a set of mappings, usually loaded from a database or configuration file. This provides a loose coupling between the View and Model that can make an application significantly easier to create and maintain.

While implementing an entire MVC architecture from scratch isn't all that simple, there are a number of reasons to do it. One reason is to ensure a clean separation between application layers at each tier. Sometimes it seems like overkill to implement additional objects, like `ValueObjects`, to pass information between layers, but in the long run it is worthwhile. Having a clean separation also makes it easier for development teams to divvy up roles and responsibilities in code, not to mention that you will find your application is much easier to maintain because as changes arise, and they always do, they will be easier to isolate without having to redo objects. That's the theory anyway, and if you stick to your guns, the theory can be put into good practice.

### 1.2.2 The Model

If you have had the pleasure of writing your own MVC-based application, you know that it can be quite a bit of work. With the Struts framework, you get the benefit of only having to plug in certain pieces. For the Model, this includes writing Action classes.

Action classes provide the business logic of your application. Typically, you want to think of Action classes as thin classes that use EJBs or Javabeans to do the actual work. The dispatch is done from the Controller to the Action class. The dispatch is determined by using an XML-based configuration file called `struts-config.xml`.

### 1.2.3 The View

The View consists of JSPs and a set of JSP custom tags that work in concert with the Controller Servlet. There is no flow logic or business logic, and no model information is contained in the View. While it isn't required that you use any of the custom tags provided by Struts in your JSPs, most situations will benefit from using them. Using the `ActionForm` (a class that we'll go into detail on later, but for now, it suffices to say that it's used to pass information from JSPs to the Model) and the tag libraries allows for a fast creation of forms for applications and also provides a built-in mechanism to use resource files for the internationalization of screens.

### 1.2.4 The Controller

The controller is a Servlet that uses the Command Design pattern to dispatch incoming requests to the appropriate Action classes. The controller Servlet, called the `ActionServlet` in the Struts framework, is configured in your web server `web.xml` and also uses the `struts-config.xml` file for determining action mappings. There actually isn't any work that needs to be done other than configuring the `web.xml` to create an instance of `org.apache.struts.action.ActionServlet`. Simple enough.

### 1.2.5 Application Model

Before we start looking at each component in detail, we can tie all the pieces together by looking at Figure 1.4.

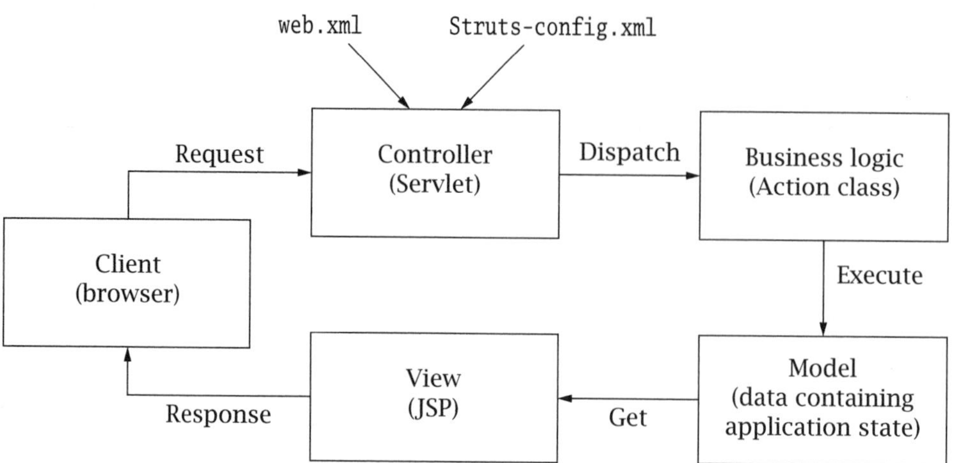


**Figure 1.4:** Application model using Struts components.

We have an HTTP request from the client browser that creates an event. The web container will eventually respond with an HTTP response. The Controller receives the request from the browser and makes the decision where to send the request. The appropriate Action class is called. The Action class uses Beans or EJBs to process the business logic and update the state of the model. The Action class is used to help control the flow of the application.

The Model represents the state of the application. The business objects update the application state. But instead of manipulating the Model, the Controller delegates this task to specialized Action classes. The Model is still implemented using JavaBeans, although they are subclasses of `ActionForm`, which are provided by the framework.

`ActionForm` Beans represent the Model state at a session (and sometimes a request level), and not at a persistent level. Session or request level means that if the container crashes, then the information held in the session or request is not recoverable. When using a persistent level concerning the Model, the current state can be recovered if the container unexpectedly has problems. A good rule of thumb is that the Model is typically going to be concerned with session state, while the Controller will be focused more on a request state. The JSP file reads information from the `ActionForm` Bean using JSP tags.

The View is simply a JSP file. In a well-designed JSP, there is no flow logic, no business logic, and no model information—there are just tags. Tags are one of the things that make Struts unique as a framework.

## 1.3 Introduction to Struts 1.1

Some of you might have already used Struts 1.0 and are looking for details on Struts 1.1. This book (and the accompanying sample application) are based on Struts 1.1. We will be discussing all these features in various chapters, so if you are brand new to Struts, then this probably won't mean much at this point. However, for those who have Struts 1.0.2 under their belts, here's a taste of the new enhancements minus the details. A number of new features have been incorporated into this release, including

- Use of Jakarta Commons libraries such as BeanUtils and Logging
- DynaActionsForms for creating dynamic action forms that do not require any coding
- Multiple application support for allowing multiple `struts-config.xml` files to be defined
- Nested tag library for allowing a nested object hierarchy to be easily accessed from JSPs
- Plugin API for `ActionServlet` enhancements
- Declarative exception handling that allows Actions to not have to worry about catching all exceptions

If you are migrating a Struts 1.0.x application to 1.1, you should not feel much pain. Some of the package names have changed since classes have been moved from the Struts utilities package into the Jakarta Commons project, so you might have to adjust your existing package or class imports. One of the nice things about Struts and the developers who contribute to the project is that there is a high degree of backward compatibility. Even though the structure of the `web.xml` and `struts-config.xml` files have had attribute and element adjustments, you can still run your 1.0.x configuration files within a 1.1 environment.

## 1.4 Moving On

In this chapter, we grounded ourselves with the necessary technologies to start using the Struts framework. These included JSP, Servlets, custom tag libraries, and XML. We also looked at the role of the web application server when using Struts applications. Struts is a framework based on the MVC design pattern. The Model components are used to maintain the state of your application, the View components are used for communicating the Model state to the presentation tier, and the Controller is used to coordinate the Model and View. Understanding these basic concepts of the MVC model is important so that you can internalize why things are done in certain ways within the Struts framework.

We should now have a baseline understanding to further our discussion. For further information and resource pointers, you can access the web site for this book at *www.mkp.com/practical/struts*.

So, with your firm understanding of the technologies involved in using Struts and a layout of how to apply MVC to your web applications, let's move on to how to develop a web application using Struts and to the details for using each of the Struts components.

chapter 2

# Framework Components Overview

When using an MVC model, and therefore when using the Struts framework, it becomes difficult to talk about various components without at least garnering a familiarity with the overall component structure. This is because inevitably we talk about one component as it relates to another. This is one of the pleasures of working with Object-Oriented technologies.

This chapter introduces the various Struts components and briefly describes what the purpose of each is. Keep in mind that we'll be going into details on the classes in the component packages in the chapters ahead, but this chapter lays the groundwork so that you can follow subsequent chapters and be familiar with the class names and their purpose, even if we haven't covered the details of a particular component.

Using combinations of all the components we are about to mention is how you will build your web applications. For a detailed look at the Struts 1.1 UML diagram, refer to Appendix A.

## 2.1 Controlling Flow with the ActionServlet Component

There is only one controller component in the Struts framework, and that is the `org.jakarta.struts.action.ActionServlet`. The `ActionServlet` represents the Controller in the MVC design pattern. Addtionally, the `ActionServlet` implements both the Front Controller and the Singleton pattern. A quick and dirty description of the Front Controller pattern is that it allows for a centralized access point for presentation-tier request handling. The Singleton pattern provides a single instance of an object and is a good sample of a pattern within a pattern.[1] There is one instance of this Servlet class per web application that receives and processes all requests that change the state of a user's interaction with the application. (Note: This is true of all other singletons within Struts.) The `ActionServlet` instance selects and invokes an Action class to perform the requested business logic. The Action classes don't produce the next page of

[1] I recommend becoming familiar with the various J2EE patterns. *Core J2EE Patterns—Best Practices and Design Strategies* by Alur, Crupi, and Malks is a must for your bookshelf.

the user interface directly; instead, they use the `RequestDispatcher.forward()` facility of the Servlet API to pass control to an appropriate JSP in order to produce the next page of the user interface. The `RequestDispatcher` object provides methods for controlling application flow without having to actually send data back to the client. The `forward()` method is a server-side transfer mechanism used to transfer control to another JSP (or Servlet for that matter).

The version of `ActionServlet` that is distributed with the framework implements the logic flow for each incoming client HTTP request. First the action is identified from the incoming request URI that was submitted by a client browser. This URI is parsed, and the substring is then used to select the appropriate action to invoke. The substring is used to map to the Java class name of the corresponding Action class. If this is the first request for a particular Action class, the class will be instantiated and will then be cached for future use by the Servlet. If an `ActionFormBean` corresponding to a View page has been specified in the configuration of the action, then the properties of that form Bean will be populated, and optionally the `validate()` method will be called on the `ActionFormBean`. The `validate()` method is used, you guessed it, to validate properties of a form. It can be used for verifying user input or to correct formatting of form fields that appear on a JSP.

There is a method in the Action class that plays an important role, and that is the `execute()` method, formerly known in the Struts 1.0.x releases as the `perform()` method. We'll talk about this method in detail when we cover Actions, but for now, the `execute()` method of this Action class is called from the `ActionServlet`. A reference to the action mapping that was used by the `ActionServlet` is passed as one of the parameters. This mapping provides access to the `ActionServlet` and `ServletContext`, as well as to other information contained in the mapping that can be used by the action itself. The `request` and `response` that were passed to the controller by the servlet container are also passed into the `execute()` method. These parameters ensure that the action has all the information it needs to complete its task.

When creating your controller Servlet, if you don't need to customize anything in your Servlet, you can simple specify in the `web.xml` file an instance of `org.apache.struts.action.ActionServlet`. It is also possible to override some or all of this functionality by sub-classing this servlet and implementing your own version of the processing. The `ActionServlet` is configured by parameters configured in the `web.xml` file. We'll discuss the available parameters in Chapter 6.

Figure 2.1 shows the flow of a request coming into the controller and how it is handled.

## 2.2 Working with the Model Components

The M in the MVC framework contains the Model components. The Model components are those focused on keeping track of the state of your application. It is here where the business logic specific to your application is maintained. Using classes provided in the Struts framework, it is possible to create your own Action components. Actions are the meat of the Struts framework. The Actions are called to perform some type of required task for the application. The Struts package that contains classes related to Action functionality is `org.apache.struts.action`. This package contains a number of classes that we will be interested in. We'll talk about

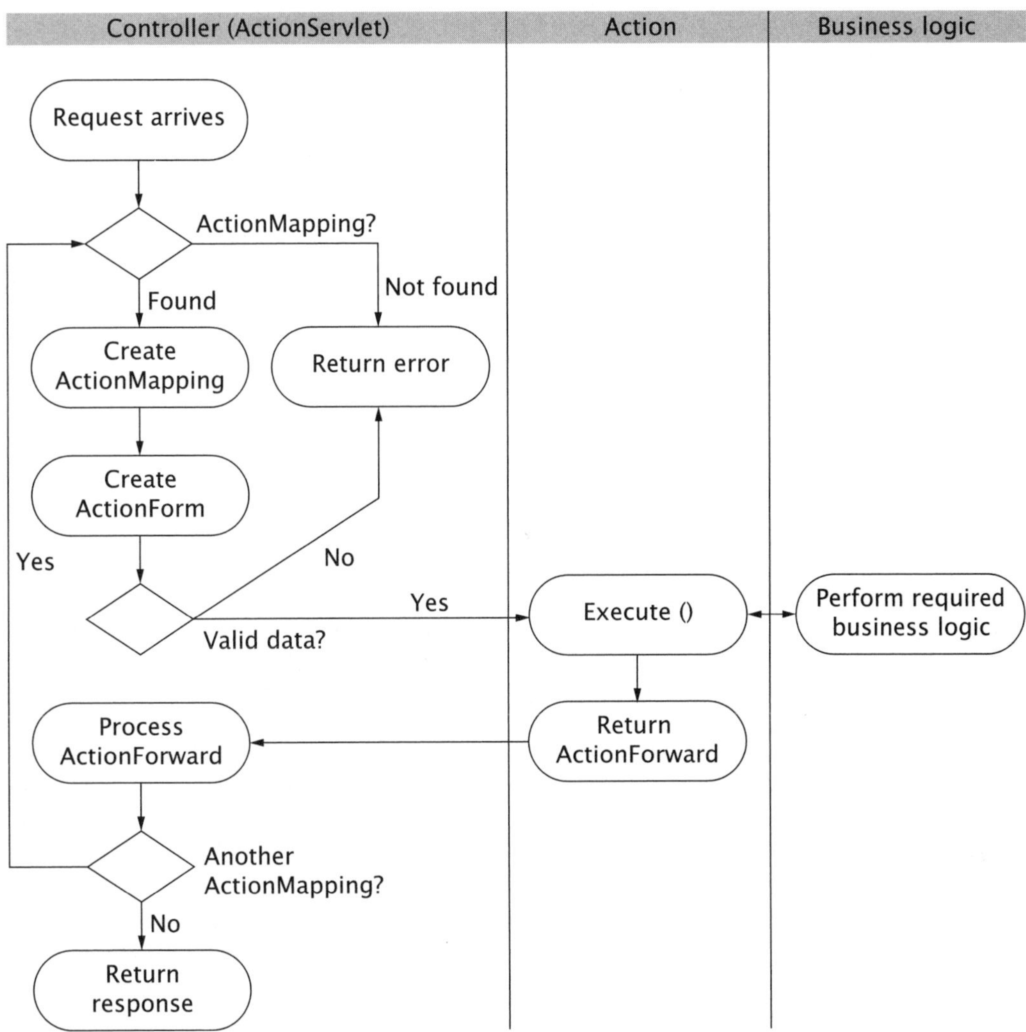


**Figure 2.1:** Request/response activity diagram.

the Action and ActionForm classes briefly here since there are entire chapters dedicated to them. Let's walk though the available classes in the action package to become familiar with them.

### 2.2.1 org.apache.struts.action.ActionMapping

The ActionServlet needs some mechanism to determine how to route requests to Action classes. This is done using an ActionMapping class. The ActionMapping represents the information that the ActionServlet knows about the mapping of a particular request to an instance of a particular Action class. The mapping is passed to the execute() method of the Action class, enabling access to this information directly. An example of how an action mapping is defined in the struts-config.xml file is

```
<action-mappings>
 <action    path="/search"
            type="cdmanager.actions.SearchAction"
            name="searchForm"
            scope="request"
            input="/search.jsp">
    <forward name="success" path="/display.jsp"/>
  </action>
</action-mappings>
```

The path property is the request URI path used to select this mapping. If extension mapping is used for the controller servlet, the extension will be stripped before comparisons against this value are made.

The type property specifies the fully qualified Java class name of the Action implementation used by this mapping.

The name property specifies the name of the form Bean if there is one associated with this Action.

The scope property identifies the scope that can be requested or the session that the form Bean (if there was one specified) creates.

The input property is the context-relative path of the input form to which control should be returned if a validation error is encountered. For example, this property is used if you have an input form that uses validation and one of the required fields is missing. The controller needs to know what to do when such a validation error occurs and is returned from the ActionForm. The input property tells the controller where to proceed next.

The forward property provides Action-local names of logical ActionForward instances that can be returned by the Action to control what does the actual presentation. The action is still called. It is possible to specify multiple forward declarations for each action. It is likely that the action can have multiple forward locations—each one with a complete set of parameters that can override those of the defaults in the associated action destination. As we proceed with our sample application, we'll see how it is also possible to forward to other actions and not just to JSPs. Doing so cuts down on the number of pages you have to create because it allows for reuse of generic pages by merely changing the generic fields on the page. For example, a title for the page can be specified in the XML for the action or by using the forward mappings. Using forward mapping is an extremely powerful Struts feature that we'll explore in more detail as this book progresses.

We'll look at the complete set of available properties in Chapter 4. If you need to add your own additional properties, it can be done by a subclassing ActionMapping and then by providing appropriate public getter and setter methods.

There is also an ActionMappings class that is found in the org.apache.struts.action package. Notice the *s* in ActionMappings; it indicates that it is a collection of some sort.

In this case, the collection is a FastHashMap. The FastHashMap is a customized implementation of java.util.HashMap designed to operate in a multithreaded environment where the majority of method calls are read-only. The ActionMappings is an implementation of a FastHashMap. FastHashMap was part of the org.apache.struts.util package but has since been moved to the Apache Commons project under the Collection classes, and can be found at *jakarta.apache.org/commons/collections.html.* ActionMappings is simply used to encapsulate a collection of ActionMapping objects that can be administered and searched. In Struts 1.1, the collections are actually stored in regular HashMaps—with no synchronization—because the configurations are frozen at startup time.

### 2.2.2 org.apache.struts.action.Action

An Action is an adapter between the contents of an incoming HTTP request and the corresponding business logic that should be executed to process it. Think of each Action as the glue between the client request and the business logic that must be performed. Actions are usually thin classes with most of the business logic being performed in a separate JavaBean or EJB.[2] The ActionServlet selects an appropriate Action for each request, creates an instance (if necessary), and calls the execute() method.

### 2.2.3 org.apache.struts.action.ActionForward

An ActionForward represents a destination that the ActionServlet might be directed to perform a RequestDispatcher.forward() or HttpServletResponse.sendRedirect(). Both of these mechanisms are used to transfer control to another JSP or Servlet. The forward does so from the server side; the sendRedirect actually sends a new URL to the client. There is a section in Chapter 6 that discusses forward vs. redirect. Which forwarding method is used is determined by the processing activities of an Action class. Instances of this class may be created dynamically as necessary by the Action class, or configured in association with an ActionMapping instance for named lookup. There are multiple potential destinations for a particular mapping instance. The Action class determines which destination should be used.

An ActionForward as specified in the struts-config.xml file might be defined within an action mapping as

```
<forward name="success" path="/display.jsp" redirect="false"/>
```

The name property defines a logical name by which this instance may be looked up in relation to a particular ActionMapping.

---

[2] The JavaBean or EJB is typically a helper class and can be considered part of a View Helpers design pattern. The View Helpers defines helper classes (which are usually Beans, EJBs, or custom tags) that store the View's intermediate data model and serve as business data adapters. Encapsulating the business logic in a helper allows for a more modular application and encourages component reuse.

The path property is the context-relative URI to which control should be forwarded, or an absolute or relative URI to which control should be redirected.

The redirect property is set to true if the ActionServlet calls HttpServletResponse.sendRedirect() on the associated path. If not specified, redirect will be false.

Why and when should you use a redirect? If you have finished handling a form submission in an Action and then forward to the next page, you might notice that the URL displayed in the web browser is the path to the previous action even though you are on a new JSP. If the previous page had a form on it and you click the browser's refresh button, you will be prompted to resubmit the form, even if the new JSP doesn't have a form on it. The way to avoid this and have the correct URL displayed is to set redirect to true as shown in the following example:

```
<forward name="success" path="/insert.jsp" redirect="true" />
```

There are two important points to consider when using redirect: performance (because of the extra client round trip), and the ability to use request attributes to communicate information from the Action to the JSP. In general, Struts developers are far better off if they can train their users to simply ignore the URL shown in the browser, or if they take additional steps—like using frames or browser windows with no location bar—to hide it.

It is also possible to use the global-forwards section in the Struts-config.xml file. Global forwards are used to create logical name mappings for commonly used JSPs so that you don't have to define the forward for each and every action mapping. A sample of the global-forwards section looks like

```
  <global-forwards>
    <forward   name="logoff"              path="/logoff.do"/>
    <forward   name="logon"               path="/logon.jsp"/>
    <forward   name="success"             path="/mainMenu.jsp"/>
</global-forwards>
```

Each of the forwards defined in the global-forwards section is available through a call to your action mapping instance, that is, actionMappingInstance.findForward("success"). Keep in mind, local <forward> elements for the same name (nested inside an <action> element) will override the global forward's normal information for that action only.

As with the ActionMapping, additional properties can be provided as needed by subclasses, and there is also an ActionForwards class that holds a collection of ActionForwards and implements the FastHashMap.

## 2.2.4 org.apache.struts.action.ActionError

The mechanism to return errors that occur during an ActionForm validation uses the ActionError class. ActionError is an encapsulation of an individual error message returned by the validate() method of an ActionForm. The error consists of a message key that is used to look up the text from the appropriate message resource file. The text in the message resource file can contain up to four placeholder objects that are used for parametric replacement in the message text. The placeholder objects are referenced in the message text using the same syntax used by the JDK MessageFormat class. Thus the first placeholder is {0}, the second is {1}, etc. The collection of ActionErrors is stored in the ActionErrors class that just provides a convenient method for accessing the ActionError stored in a java.util.HashMap. This HashMap is the accumulated set of ActionError objects for each property, keyed by property name. If you want to know all the fancy stuff you can do with message format strings, reference the java.text.MessageFormat API.

Validation errors either are global to the entire ActionForm Bean they are associated with or are specific to a particular Bean property and the error corresponds to a specific input field on the corresponding form. If we take a look at the validate() method in one of our ActionForms, we see how errors are processed.

```
public ActionErrors validate(ActionMapping mapping,
                             HttpServletRequest request) {

        ActionErrors errors = new ActionErrors();
        if (
              ((title == null) ||  (title.length() < 1))
              &&((artist == null)||  (artist.length() < 1))
              &&((genre == null) ||  (genre.length() < 1))
              )
            errors.add("search", new ActionError("error.searchcriteria.required"));
        return errors;
    }
```

In this particular validate() method, we create an instance of ActionErrors. The collection is empty unless our validation criteria fail. If we must add an error, we create a new instance of an ActionError with the message key and add it to our collection using search as the key. When the JSP displays the page, having the Struts <html:errors> tag placed on the page like

```
<html:errors/>
```

will cause any errors to be displayed to the user.

### 2.2.5 org.apache.struts.action.ActionMessage

The ActionMessage (and ActionMessages) work exactly the same way as the ActionError (and ActionErrors). ActionMessages are new to Struts 1.1. The difference is that an ActionMessage can be used to pass messages that *aren't* errors. This is useful when you have, for example, a confirmation page where you want to just display a generic or informational message to the user. Rather than having a separate JSP to forward that displays the results, you can include a message that is displayed on the JSP. The following code could be included in an Action class:

```
ActionMessages actionMessages = new ActionMessages();
actionMessages.add(ActionMessages.GLOBAL_MESSAGE,
                   new ActionMessage("record.inserted"));
saveMessages(request,actionMessages);
```

Then to retrieve the message, the JSP uses the following tags. Setting the message attribute to true in the <logic:messagePresent> and <html:messages> tells the tag to look for ActionMessages instead of ActionErrors.

```
<logic:messagesPresent message="true">
<tr>
  <html:messages id="message" message="true">
  <td><bean:write name="message"/></td>
  </html:messages>
</tr>
</logic:messagesPresent>
```

## 2.3 View Components

Since we are exploring the various components provided in the MVC model, we should be fair and include all the components. The View components consist of the following: the JSPs you create specific to your application and the ActionForm, which is an optional JavaBean associated with a form on your JSP. The custom tag libraries provided with Struts are also used within your JSPs and can be considered View components. One of the many features of using the custom tag libraries is that you can repopulate fields in your JSPs easily. However, since we spend a number of detailed chapters on the custom tag libraries, the tag libraries are only casually mentioned here. Let's look at the ActionForm class.

### 2.3.1 org.apache.struts.action.ActionForm

For each JSP that has input data entry requirements, it is possible to have an ActionForm. An ActionForm is a JavaBean optionally associated with one or more ActionMappings. Such a Bean will have had its properties initialized from the corresponding request parameters before the corresponding action's execute() method is called.

When the properties of this Bean have been populated, but before the execute() method of the Action is called, this Bean's validate() method is called, which gives the Bean a chance to verify that the properties submitted by the user are correct and valid. This is done only if the Bean has requested validation as specified in the struts-config.xml file. If this method finds problems, it returns an error messages object that encapsulates those problems, and the controller servlet returns control to the corresponding input form. Otherwise, the validate() method returns null, indicating that everything is acceptable and the corresponding Action's execute() method should be called.

This class must be subclassed in order to be instantiated. Subclasses should provide property getter and setter methods for all the Bean properties they wish to expose plus override any of the public or protected methods that they wish to provide modified functionality for.

## 2.4 Summary

Chapter 2 has provided a glimpse at the basic components provided in the Struts framework and touched on some of the tags provided in the Struts tag library. It introduced the various classes provided in the Struts packages so that you can start becoming familiar with the classes we will be working with. These include the Controller component `org.jakarta.struts.action.ActionServlet` as well as numerous Model components. All the Model components can be found in the `org.jakarta.struts.action` package. The View portion of the framework contains the JSP files that a page author will write specific to an application, the custom tag libraries, as well as to the `ActionForm` component. Using these components as our groundwork, we can now examine in detail how to apply them in your web application development. This is where the fun starts.

chapter 3

# Struts Development Plan

This chapter examines a sensible development plan that can be applied to most projects, regardless of size, that use Struts. In the following pages, we will create the development plan that this book will use to build and demonstrate each Struts component in detail.

This isn't a "preaching from on high" development plan; it is merely a suggestion. If you have a well-defined plan for approaching MVC model development that works for you, then stick with it. Please note that this is not meant to define your development process. So whether you follow the Rational Unified Process (RUP) or an Extreme Programming (XP) paradigm, or any other methodology, it's all good. What's presented here is more a suggested outline of appropriate steps to take when laying out your Struts project so that you can build applications quickly. I call it the "Ten-Step Development Program."

The process presented here is the one that I use in my own production development projects, and it can be directly applied to any application using the Struts framework. I think it will prove helpful for many readers. At the very least, it provides another point of view to those who already have their own development plans in place. Please note that although we are using pieces of this development program throughout the book, we will not be following it step by step in each chapter so that the material follows a more natural flow to enhance efforts to learn it.

## 3.1 The Premise

When using any technology, the first question that you should always ask yourself is "Why should I use this technology?" Though there are any number of responses that could satisfactorily answer this question, somewhere in the answer should be that the technology in question solves a problem for you. What the answer should *not* include is that the technology is just the next whiz-bang tech-toy getting lots of airtime, although I'm sure we're all guilty of considering that a satisfactory reason for using a new technology at some point in our careers.

You might ask why any of the precious page count allowed for this book is being used to talk about a development plan approach, and it's a valid question. The reason we're talking about a plan is I'm a firm believer in not wasting time. We will walk through a development project in order to familiarize you with the thought process and layout of the various Struts components. Doing it in this fashion can also easily be applied to larger, more complex projects. Breaking down the steps eliminates a lot of wasted cycles in the learning process. It also eliminates a lot of wasted cycles in your actual development when you start coding.

So again, as a developer, architect, or manager, when you select a technology to solve a problem, you need to know what the problem is you're trying to solve, and you need to know if your chosen technology is up to the task. Struts can solve a whole lot of problems; just be sure that they are the ones you need solved. If it seems that Struts is a good solution, then I can say without reservation that it's a framework you should consider. But just because you are reading this book doesn't mean that Struts is a good fit for the project you're thinking of applying it to. Make sure you think that through before you start.

Remember that when dealing with any framework, there is a ramp-up time that has to be considered, and Struts is no exception. If you do decide to use Struts, though, your ramp-up time will be dramatically reduced—assuming that I do my job well writing this book.

## 3.2 Identify the Applicability

Before starting on the actual project development plan, be sure that Struts applies to your project. If it does, you will answer the following questions with a solid yes. If more than a couple of the answers are no or maybe, then you should reconsider if Struts is really your best tool.

- Does this project have many screens?
- Are there a lot of interactions required from the user?
- Is it important to have flexible configuration?
- Does this application fit into the MVC model?
- Are the roles and responsibilities of the development team clearly defined?

The last question addresses a common scenario. Most development projects that I have been a part of separate the frontend engineers from the backend engineers because they require different skill sets. The frontend engineers are the experts at HTML, JavaScript, DHTML, etc. The backend engineers are the people writing the Java code and interacting with the business model. Struts allows for a clear separation of development roles and makes it easy to split tasks between the frontend and backend teams. However, in very small development teams, it's not unheard of for one or two people to perform both frontend and backend work.

## 3.3 Ten-Step Development Program

I've broken the plan into ten logical steps. It's acknowledged that some of the terms about to be used might not yet be familiar to you, but hang in there. After you've had a chance to work your way through the whole book, revisit this chapter. The light bulbs might flash brighter after you've absorbed all the Struts internals. In the meantime, it certainly won't hurt to get your feet firmly placed on the ground before we dive into those internals.

First, let's look at the steps and talk a bit more about each one and why it is important. Then we can start to apply each to our sample project.

1. Gather and define the application requirements.
2. Define and develop each screen requirement in terms of the data collected and/or displayed.
3. Determine all the access paths for each screen.
4. Define the `ActionMappings` that correlate to the application business logic.
5. Create the `ActionForms` with defined properties from the screen requirements (this can include the validation portions as well).
6. Develop Actions to be called by the `ActionMappings` that, in turn, call the appropriate helpers and forward to JSPs.
7. Develop the application business logic (Beans, EJBs, etc.).
8. Create JSPs to match the workflows using the `ActionMappings`.
9. Build the appropriate configuration files; this includes `struts-config.xml` and `web.xml`.
10. Build, test, deploy.

Let's look at each step in more detail by referring to the specific sample application we will use throughout this book.

## 3.4 Gather and Define the Application Requirements

While "gather and define the application requirements" might be a perfectly logical statement, for those of us who live and work in the real world, it is one that is commonly overlooked in favor of just building something . . . building anything. And this "fools rush in" approach typically leads to building the wrong thing. It pays in both time and sanity to make the effort to completely understand your requirements. This step works well in conjunction with Use Case diagrams if you are creating them for your project.

The application that we'll build in this book is a direct result of my bad memory. I have a rather large CD music collection that currently has no organization to it. In fact, I've purchased duplicate CDs more than once, which is embarrassing, but I did it because I didn't realize I already owned those CDs. So I decided to build a CD Manager application to maintain my CD collection. Truthfully, I want to demonstrate a fairly simple application that uses most (if not all) of the Struts 1.1 features so you can see how they shine. I also have had my fill of the ubiquitous "Hello World" and "Shopping Cart" samples. So now for something completely different.

Let's define the requirements. The CD Manager must

- Provide a secure logon mechanism.
- Add a new CD.
- Search for a CD when given search criteria.
- Display a list of CDs.
- Logoff from the application.

This simple set of tasks helps us define our user displays, or forms, as well as the "what has to happen when a user clicks a button," also known as the actions. These requirements also reveal a couple of other details. For instance, we need a way to store data. The database interaction for this application is discussed briefly in Section 3.10. But be aware that building a database is not the focus of this book. Refer to the book's companion web site for details about getting your database downloaded and set up.

## 3.5 Define and Develop Each Screen Requirement

After the first glance at the CD Manager, it looks like we will have four screens: logon, insert, search, display. We don't need a separate screen for logging off since that is just an action and there is no additional data required to do it. But if we think this program through a bit more, we find that we need a way to access the various functions, and so we need a Main Menu screen as well. That makes five screens. The data required from the user for each screen is shown in Table 3.1.

**Table 3.1:** Screen requirements.

| Screen | Data fields | Type | Comments |
|---|---|---|---|
| Logon | Username | String | Editable |
| | Password | String | Editable |
| Insert | Title, Artist, Genre | String | Editable |
| Search | Title, Artist, Genre | String | Editable |
| Display | Title, Artist, Genre | String | Read-only |
| Main Menu | None | | Contains only hyperlinks to other screens including logoff action |

## 3.6 Determine All the Access Paths for Each Screen

We want to define, as best we can, how each screen will be accessed. This step is helpful in starting a logic flow for an application, especially if you are working with a large number of screens.

In our simple application this step is easy; but in applications with a large number of screens, looking at your screen access definitions can quickly start to remind you of a plate of spaghetti.

While it is possible to model screen accesses using UML tools, I tend to go back to basics with this one by using a tool that is commonly overlooked called Paperware. Write the screen name on a Post-it note, and use a whiteboard. You can easily move the Post-its and draw lines for the screen access. After you've got something that is workable, go back and then put it into a project artifact, like a screen model in UML. I just find that it's much quicker to do it this way.

This step also helps to identify if there are any screens missing, or if there are any that can be logically combined. By determining all screen accesses, you will be forced to think through how the application will logically flow. More than likely, there will be adjustments necessary at this juncture. This is a healthy point to start seeing what an application will look like. We can start to see the layout of our screen access by the activity diagram shown in Figure 3.1.

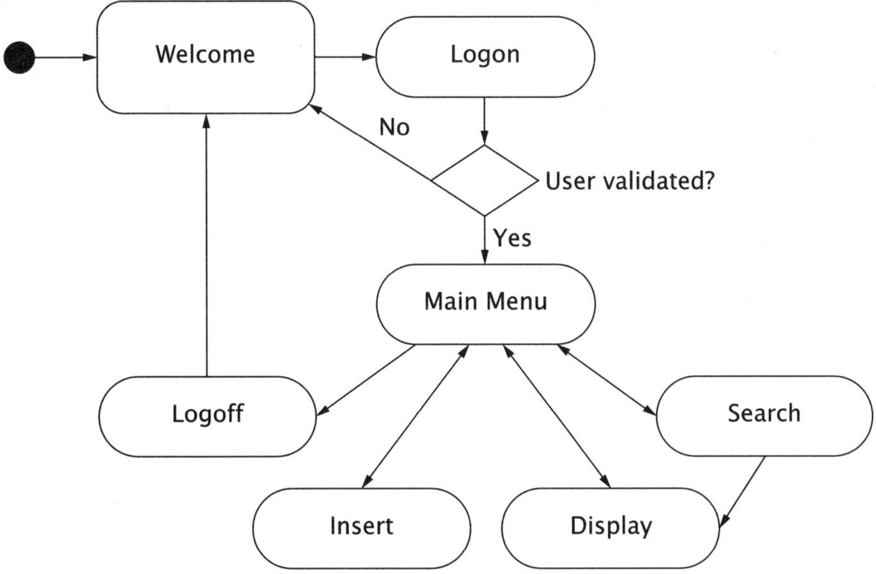


**Figure 3.1:** CD Manager activity diagram.

## 3.7 Define the ActionMappings

We can see that once we have determined how the screen accesses take place, the next logical step is to determine what happens when the screen is actually accessed. This is where the `ActionMapping` plays a role. Think of the `ActionMappings` as a roadmap and the Actions as the vehicles. The `ActionMappings` determine the roadway to be taken by the Actions. We have more details coming up that clarify this, so for now it's sufficient to say that the `ActionMappings` determine what twists and turns are allowed. In defining an `ActionMapping`, it is necessary to determine what happens upon the successful completion, failure, or any other process that needs to be initiated from the resulting Action class.

## 3.8 Create the ActionForms

Create the `ActionForms` with defined properties from the screen requirements (this can include the validation portions as well). All form classes in Struts extend `org.apache.struts.action.ActionForm` or `org.apache.struts.action.DynaActionForm`. `DynaActionForms` are those forms that handle dynamic definitions of properties. More of this discussion is held off until later in the book. For now, as long as you are comfortable with the `ActionForm` class, everything's okay.

The Form class is used to correspond to the data fields on a screen. The `ActionForm` is used to transfer data from a JSP and make it available in an Object form that should correlate the data fields that we defined in step two when we developed our screen requirements.

The Form class is also used for validation of form fields. Validation can be performed for requirement of fields, syntax of fields, or limitations of certain fields. The Setter/Getter (accessor/mutator) methods are called automatically on an HTML form submit, thereby being available to the Action class for future use. Usually, an `ActionForm` class handles all the variables on a form and has the necessary validation for a specific screen. I tend to keep all of my Form and Action classes in separate packages; otherwise, it can get too confusing once you get more than a couple of screens in place.

Not every screen requires an `ActionForm`. In our CD Manager, we have only three `ActionForms`: Logon, Insert, and Search. Our Main Menu screen doesn't have any fields on it other than hyperlinks. Since we spend a chapter on `ActionForms`, we will go into more detail about this there.

## 3.9 Develop Actions

The next step in the process is to develop the Actions necessary in our application. We can look at information from the previous steps to define what has to happen in each Action. In fact, the `ActionMappings` should tell us primarily what Actions must be constructed. Remember, the `ActionMappings` are like the roadmap, so they tell us how we get from point A to point B. An Action will take place for each situation, or activity, possible in the application. If we identify our Actions for the CD Manager, we have

- *LogonAction.* Once the user logs on, compares the username and password to those in a database. If the username and password match, then the activity returns success; otherwise, the result is a failure.
- *InsertAction.* Takes the necessary information from the JSP and inserts a new record into the database. If the insert is successful, then we will display a message; otherwise, a failure will be returned.
- *SearchAction.* Returns the records that match given criteria. The user and what is typed in the various fields from the JSP determine the criteria. The search action will build the necessary criteria and issue a SQL request. Upon success, the `DisplayAllAction` will be called to display the records returned in the record set.
- *DisplayAllAction.* Displays the current record set.
- *LogoffAction.* Performs the necessary steps to log the current user off the system, including invalidating any session information, as well as out of the session itself.

## 3.10 Develop the Application Business Logic

The application business logic is the core of your application. Typically, your business logic is written as JavaBeans or Enterprise JavaBeans (EJB). The JavaBean or EJB is called from the appropriate Action class. For our CD Manager application, I've decided not to introduce other tangential technologies unless absolutely necessary. JavaBeans and EJBs are worth an entire book on their own. I will note in the code where you would want to separate the logic into a separate Bean.

I've included our business logic within JavaBeans that are called from the Action classes. In some places, the business logic is in the Action class. When this was done, it was done purely for the reason of keeping the application simple and making a point, not to encourage business logic in the Actions. The business logic in our application includes the access to the database. No groans, please. While I realize that I should point out the tier separation between the logic and data access layers, to do so would be beyond the scope of this book and the point of the CD Manager sample. So let's keep it simple in order to concentrate on the Struts-specific pieces.

Sometimes it's helpful to stub out the business logic when first putting an application structure together. This makes it possible to actually debug the application flow first, and then concentrate on the application business logic. In practice, this might be forcing some specific return codes so that you can execute various code paths, but it will at least get the majority of the debugging out of the way. Then you can fill in the blanks in each of the areas of the business logic.

## 3.11 Create JSPs

Next, we identify the necessary JavaServer Pages. We do this by looking back at our workflow and seeing what success, failure, or forward pages are necessary. This can be easily itemized

**Table 3.2:** JSP definitions.

| JSP | Purpose |
|---|---|
| `index.jsp` | User logon form, as well as the page to use when logging off |
| `login.jsp` | Username/password form |
| `mainMenu.jsp` | Choices available for the user to select desired action |
| `search.jsp` | Provide the search criteria form |
| `display.jsp` | Provide the display of the records returned from a record set |
| `insert.jsp` | Provide the fields needed to insert a new record into the database |
| `insertConf.jsp` | Confirm a successful insertion |

by looking back at your `ActionMappings` that were defined in the earlier step. Since the `ActionMappings` provide the roadmap, all the roads must be defined. Each success, failure, error, or other action that is a result of the Action class should be defined in your `ActionMapping`. It is possible, and quite probable, that there will be many forwards defined from various Actions. Most of the forwards will probably be JSP files, but it's not uncommon for actions to forward to another Action class.

Table 3.2 shows the JSP files for our application.

## 3.12 Build the Appropriate Configuration Files

The (almost) last step is to build the configuration files necessary for the application. Chapter 6 talks about the specifics of this, but here's a primer. The `web.xml` is used by the Servlet container to determine the configuration of the various Servlets supported on that server. The `struts-config.xml` file is used by the controller servlet (as defined in the `web.xml`) to declare `ActionForms`, `ActionClasses`, and the `ActionMappings`. It is possible to piece your `struts-config.xml` file together from the various components that we've already been building in our development process. This is one way to do so. In large-scale applications, however, where there can be many screens and actions, this is very tedious.

One way to utilize development tools and make the development process more efficient is to try to automate the process of generating the `struts-config.xml` file. This is done by using another helpful open source project called XDoclet. XDoclet is a generic Java tool that allows you to create custom Javadoc @tags. These @tags can be used to generate configuration files, like your `struts-config.xml` file, from source code. XDoclet is comprised of tasks and subtasks. `<strutsconfigxml />` is a subtask of the `<webdoclet />` task. Used in concert with the ANT build file, the task parses the source directories for Action and Form classes that contain `@struts:` tags and generates a `struts-config.xml` based on that data. For more information, refer to XDoclet at *xdoclet.sourceforge.net/*.

Another tool to consider is the Struts Console written by James Holmes. This tool lets you visually edit your `struts-config.xml` file as well as convert pages such as HTM, HTML, and

JSP to use the Struts HTML tag library for form handling. You can find the Struts Console at *www.jamesholmes.com/struts/console/.*

## 3.13 Build, Test, Deploy

The last step is to build, test, and deploy the application. Well, I guess one could argue that these are actually three steps, but in a utopian world, one would build, test, and deploy all in one step. It never hurts to dream. In this step, we use our ANT build, and various testing and logging approaches. Once we have our application debugged and tested, we deploy it on the given server as a web archive file (WAR file). We will walk through these steps in Chapter 10.

## 3.14 Summary

In this chapter, we've seen how to apply a logical development plan to an application that will use the Struts framework. This development plan is not intended to replace existing development methodologies you might already be using. Instead, it is meant to focus on the tasks that are required for building Struts applications. These steps include

1. Gather and define the application requirements.
2. Define and develop each screen requirement in terms of the data collected and/or displayed.
3. Determine all the access paths for each screen.
4. Define the `ActionMappings` that correlate to the application business logic.
5. Create the `ActionForms` with defined properties from the screen requirements (this can include the validation portions as well).
6. Develop Actions to be called by the `ActionMappings` that, in turn, call the appropriate helpers and forward to JSPs.
7. Develop the application business logic (Beans, EJBs, etc.).
8. Create JSPs to match the workflows using the `ActionMappings`.
9. Build the appropriate configuration files; this includes the `struts-config.xml` and `web.xml`.
10. Build, test, deploy.

We identified our sample application as the CD Manager that we'll use throughout the rest of the book, and we started planning our development of that application.

chapter 4

# Creating and Building Actions

This chapter walks through the creation of Struts Action classes and shows how they are used.

An Action is defined as a logical request that takes place in your web application. All the following examples are Actions: logging on, performing a search, displaying a listing, and logging off. Think of an Action as the pipe, or adapter, between the contents of an incoming HTTP request and the corresponding business logic that should be executed to process the request.

The controller (`ActionServlet`) will select an appropriate Action for each request based on the `ActionMappings` provided in the `struts-config.xml` file, create an instance of the Action (if necessary), and then call the `execute()` method of the Action.

It's important to mention that when programming Actions, they must be thread-safe. Not making them thread-safe is probably one of the most common errors programmers working with Action classes make. The reason for this is the controller shares the same instance for multiple simultaneous requests. This means you must be aware of the following "gotchas."

Instance and static variables should not, I repeat, *not* be used to store information related to the state of a particular request. That's because they are accessed through object references of the class. It's safe to use local variables because they are created on the stack that is assigned to each request thread. The stack is managed by the Java Virtual Machine (JVM) so there is no need to worry about sharing local variables between threads. The following is an example of what you should try to avoid doing by using an instance variable for a Locale object:

```
public final class LogonAction extends AbstActionBase {
      Locale locale = null;
      Public void LogonAction(){}
...
}
```

The correct way to do this would be to make locale a local variable to a method.

```
public final class LogonAction extends AbstActionBase {
      public void LogonAction(){}
```

```
        public ActionForward execute(ActionMapping mapping,
                             ActionForm form,
                             HttpServletRequest request,
                             HttpServletResponse response)
        throws Exception {
              // This is an example of a local variable
              // and would typically be followed by code as
              // indicated by the ... in this sample
              Locale locale=null;
              ...
         }
   ...
   }
```

Access to other resources such as JavaBeans or session variables must be synchronized if those resources require protection. Most resource classes are generally designed to provide their own protection when necessary, but you should be aware of all this if you are dealing with issues surrounding synchronization.

When an Action instance is first created, the controller servlet calls `setServlet()` with a non-null argument to identify the controller servlet instance to which this Action is attached. When the controller servlet is to be shut down (or restarted), the `setServlet()` method is called with a null argument that can be used to clean up any allocated resources in use by this Action.

With all this under our belt, let's build our Logon action from scratch.

## 4.1 Creating an Action

For each logical request, we write an Action class. This starts by extending `org.apache.struts.action.Action`.

```
import org.apache.struts.action.Action;
public final class LogonAction extends Action {}
```

While it is perfectly fine to have each of your Action classes extend the `org.apache.struts.action.Action` class, I prefer to define a base Action class for the application. The reason is that it is common to have many Actions defined in a web application. It is also typical that these Actions have a number of methods that they all have to perform. This can vary from application to application.

To enforce the contract between the base class and any subclasses, make the base class `abstract`. Each of the classes that extends the base class must implement its own version of the `execute()` method, so the `execute()` method in the base class is abstract, making the entire class abstract. There are various ways you can code this.

Another way is to declare the `execute()` method in the base class and have it call another `abstract` method, such as `performAction()`. Then each derived class would implement `performAction()` instead. The reason you'd consider doing this is if you have some type of logging code that is common to all Actions that you would like in your base class. Both ways are perfectly acceptable—it's really a matter of personal coding preference. I've chosen to make the `execute()` method abstract in the base class, but I've also included code to demonstrate both ways in the code download sample.

It's typical that an Action class will work in conjunction with EJB session Beans (or just JavaBeans).[1] These Beans contain the business logic for your application so that your project maintains a clean separation of tiers. A common method that you might need in your Action class is to get the Java Naming and Directory Interface (JNDI) context, get an instance of the context, and then do a lookup on the given JNDI name for the EJB you are interested in to retrieve the home interface. This is something that you can have in an Action base class.

Let's create the Action base class that we'll use throughout our Actions in our sample application.

```
import org.apache.struts.action.Action;
public abstract class AbstActionBase extends Action{
        ...
}
```

Our `LogonAction` then becomes

```
public final class LogonAction extends AbstActionBase {}
```

We include all of our Action classes in a common package called `cdmanager.actions`. I like to keep my Actions and Forms in separate packages. In a large-scale application, the number of Actions and Forms can quickly grow. It becomes confusing to have them mixed within the same package. I like keeping my packages clearly defined. Therefore, all of our Actions for the CD Manager application will be in `cdmanager.actions`, and all the ActionForms will be in the `cdmanager.forms` package. An alternative strategy common to larger applications is to put the form Beans and actions for logical subsets of the functionality in the same package. One advantage of doing this is that they can share package private methods without fear of possible interference if they are declared public.

## 4.2 Execute Method

The method of interest in the Struts 1.1 Action class is `execute(...)`. The execute method is called from the controller servlet when the Action is to be executed. For those familiar with Struts prior to the 1.1 release, the `perform` method was the method of interest. However, to handle declarative exception handling (which we'll talk about later in this chapter), the method signature changed slightly. The `perform` method will still be called by the Action class for backward compatibility, but if you are writing new applications, use the `execute` method.

---

[1] You should evaluate whether or not it is necessary to use EJBs in your application. Sometimes it is appropriate to use just JavaBeans and implement a Data Access Object pattern to do so. To go into the pros and cons of each approach would be beyond the scope of this book.

Execute comes in two flavors.

```
public ActionForward execute(ActionMapping mapping,
                             ActionForm form,
                             ServletRequest request,
                             ServletResponse response)
  throws java.lang.Exception;
```

and

```
public ActionForward execute(ActionMapping mapping,
                             ActionForm form,
                             HttpServletRequest request,
                             HttpServletResponse response)
  throws java.lang.Exception;
```

Usually, the `HttpServletRequest` signature version is the one that is used by the Servlet environment. Even though we haven't talked about the `ActionForward`, `ActionMapping`, or `ActionForm` in detail yet, let's take a minute to look at the method signature. This will give you an idea of the type of information available in the `execute` method. There are more details provided about each of these objects later on, but here's an overview for now.

The return type of the `ActionForward` object tells the controller where it should forward. Usually, this is another JSP, but it can also be to another Action.

The first parameter we see is the `ActionMapping` object. This is just an object representation of what is defined for this action in the `struts-config.xml` file. Remember that this config file is used by the controller to determine all the attributes of an action. The `ActionMapping` is provided so that if the Action itself needs to access any of the information concerning its configuration, it can. This is also a mechanism for providing any initialization parameters that an action might want.

The next parameter is the `ActionForm`. This object contains the fields that have been declared on a JSP form. The `ActionForm` is a JavaBean that is also used for validation, but we'll talk about how that is accomplished in Chapter 5. Briefly, the `ActionForm` Bean is created and populated with data relative to the current request. This is done by the `ActionServlet`.

The action accesses any fields that it needs to determine which business logic should take place. For example, our `LogonAction` needs to get the username and password from the Logon screen so it would do the following:

```
if (form != null){
      userName = ((LogonForm) form).getUserName();
      password = ((LogonForm) form).getPassword();
}
```

The accessor methods of the form are used to get the appropriate property. The `LogonAction` can then use these variables to do a task, such as a user authentication.

The next two parameters are the `HttpServletRequest` and `HttpServletResponse`. It is quite likely that information will be required from the incoming request. For example, we want to save an attribute in the user's session so that we can determine if the user is currently logged in or not. This would be done like so:

```
// Save our logged-in user in the session
HttpSession session = request.getSession();
session.setAttribute(Globals.USER_KEY, user);
```

Here we use our incoming request to get a session. If a session doesn't already exist, then the container will create a new one. We then set an attribute that will be used by other Actions to check for a valid user session.

Another common approach is to route all control through an Action; let the Action check for a valid session and then just forward to the JSP. In taking this approach, you can have a single continue Action that can be used for any page that doesn't require any other preprocessing. So the Action would simply have

```
return mapping.findForward(Globals.CONTINUE);
```

Personally, I prefer to have each Action check for a valid session if it needs to, as opposed to the latter approach of automatically routing through an authorization Action for each request.

## 4.3 Execution Steps in Execute

There are some common steps that are followed in the execute method. Let's look at what they are.

First, there is usually a check to make sure that you are working with a current user session. You don't want someone to be able to bookmark a page for an Action while they are logged into an application and come back at a later time when they are logged out. This would be a serious security risk.

It also could happen that someone leaves their browser inactive and their session times out. The way to avoid this type of access from happening is to have a check (another good method for the base class) for an active session. If the session is not valid, then the request can be forwarded back to a Logon JSP, preventing the user from accessing anything further. In our `AbstActionBase`, we have an `isSessionValid` method to accomplish this task. The code looks like this.

```
public boolean isSessionValid(HttpServletRequest request){
      if (request == null) return (false);
      HttpSession session = request.getSession();
      if (session == null) return(false);
      // Checked for a currently logged on user
      User user = (User) session.getAttribute(Constants.USER_KEY);
      return ((user == null) ? false : true);
}
```

We will call this method the first step in each execute(). If we have a request, then we try to retrieve the session from it. After making sure that we in fact have a session, we check to see if we have a session attribute set for the USER_KEY. The USER_KEY object is set when the user logs in. Therefore, if the attribute is not set in the session, it indicates an invalid session.

We do a quick check to see if we have a user object and return the appropriate Boolean response. However, because we are dealing with the LogonAction in this case, we don't want to check for a valid session because we haven't set it yet. If it is necessary to access various scoped objects, it's done now. For example, the Application object is in the ServletContext and can be accessed from inside an Action via the ServletConfig or HttpSession.

```
Object attribute = getServlet().getServletContext().getAttribute("attribute_name");
```

You can also just define a convenient getter method in your abstract base class for this type of requirement.

The next step typically taken is to retrieve any information, or properties, necessary from the ActionForm. Additional validation can be accomplished if it wasn't already done by the ActionForm validate() method. If any errors are found, we store the error message. This is accomplished by using the ApplicationResource file that contains message keys and accompanying messages. We'll talk more about the ApplicationResource file when we discuss internationalization in Chapter 9.

We store the error by adding the message key into an ActionErrors collection. Let's look at how we check our username/password from our LogonAction class. First, we create a collection of ActionErrors in case we have an error occur that we need to send back to the View.

```
// Validate the request parameters specified by the user
      ActionErrors errors = new ActionErrors();
```

Next we check to make sure that we have a valid ActionForm passed into the execute method. Then we pull out the appropriate properties we are interested in. In this case, those are the username and password.

```
if (form != null){
      userName = ((LogonForm) form).getUserName();
      password = ((LogonForm) form).getPassword();
}
```

Using an XML file to read as a Hashtable into a local variable database (the details of this code are presented in the code sample download), we get the User object from the database and compare the password in the database to the password entered by the user on the logon form.

```
user = (User) database.get(userName);
if ((user != null) && !user.getPassword().equals(password)){
        user = null;
   }
```

If the password doesn't match, we add an ActionError to our errors collection. We use the ActionErrors.GLOBAL_ERROR property name marker to indicate that this is a global error and not one related to a specific property on the form.[2]

```
if (user == null)
    errors.add(ActionErrors.GLOBAL_ERROR, new ActionError("error.password.mismatch"));
}
```

Then we check to see if our errors collection contains any errors. If so, we call the saveErrors method of the Action. Doing so will save the specified error message keys into the appropriate request attribute for use by the errors custom tag. If any messages were set, they will be displayed in the View. Otherwise, the saveErrors method ensures that the request attribute is not created. Make sure that you include a call to saveErrors. Otherwise, if you had errors pending to be displayed, they won't be set. Also note that the mapping.getInput() method call is getting the value of the input attribute as defined in the ActionMapping for this Action so the controller knows where to forward to next.

```
// Report any errors we have discovered back to the original form
if (!errors.empty()) {
       saveErrors(request, errors);
       return (new ActionForward(mapping.getInput()));
}
```

After we've determined that no errors occurred with the form properties, we can determine what necessary business logic must take place. While it is possible to do this through logic code within the Action class, it is preferable—and is a better application design practice—to have a business Bean handle this and then just call the appropriate method in the Bean. Doing this better adheres to the Model separation of MVC.

In our LogonAction, our logic is not all that interesting. We want to save the user as a session variable so that we know we have a logged-on user and can possibly log an appropriate message to our Servlet log file. We'll talk in more detail about how to use the Logging provided in Struts 1.1 in Chapter 11, but a simple introduction to logging is included here.

To demonstrate this simple example, I'm using the servlet.log() method. Next, depending on the results of our business logic, we might or might not need to save information into the server-side objects. This information is used by the next page or JSP. Usually, something is set in either the request or the session scope.

```
// Save our logged-in user in the session
HttpSession session = request.getSession();
session.setAttribute(Globals.USER_KEY, user);
if (servlet.getDebug() >= 1)
    servlet.log("LogonAction: User [" + user.getUserName() +
                "] logged on in session " + session.getId());
```

---

[2] The dot notation used when new'ing the ActionError is referencing the key from the ApplicationResource file. We will discuss this in Chapter 9.

After we've completed all the activities in our Action, the last step is to determine what the next page—or the forward—should be. The forward uses the ActionForward object and represents a destination to which the controller servlet might be directed to perform a RequestDispatcher.forward() or HttpServletResponse.sendRedirect() to another JSP. That JSP will then be used to generate a response based on the information in the updated Beans.

The ActionForward can be instantiated either (1) dynamically as necessary by using

```
new ActionForward(String path) or
new ActionForward(String path, boolean redirect)
```

(2) by being configured in association with an ActionMapping instance for a logical named path lookup like

```
ActionForward actionForward =
mapping.findForward(Globals.FORWARD_SUCCESS);
```

By following this general flow, it's possible to maintain clean Action classes.

## 4.4 When Bad Things Happen to Good Actions

No matter how hard we try, eventually something will go wrong. That is just a fact of life for engineers. A good engineer will therefore always have a plan for handling exceptions. It is highly likely that the Beans that represent the Model of your system may throw exceptions. This can be due to problems accessing databases or other resources. It is good practice to trap all such exceptions in the logic of the execute() method, and log them to the application log file along with the corresponding stack trace. This can be done by calling

```
servlet.log("An error occurred: ", exception);
```

### 4.4.1 ActionErrors

At first glance, you might be tempted to create custom exceptions for everything that can go wrong in the Model and then pass these exceptions through the Action class to the JSP. The JSP can then handle exceptions by cross-referencing exception types to a message key. The user then gets an error message in their native language. The problem with this is that you will most likely have a large number of custom exceptions and will probably cause maintainability issues down the road. Here's a better approach.

In most cases, exceptions can be converted to ActionErrors and then passed back to the View. If we think back to our MVC model, taking this approach keeps the messages and the message keys in the Model. The controller simply transfers the data to the View to maintain the tier separation. It's also possible to pass the entire exception back to the View by using a known attribute key in the request. This is exactly how the Struts JSP tags do it for the ActionErrors. Figure 4.1 shows a sequence diagram demonstrating how an error is actually handled.

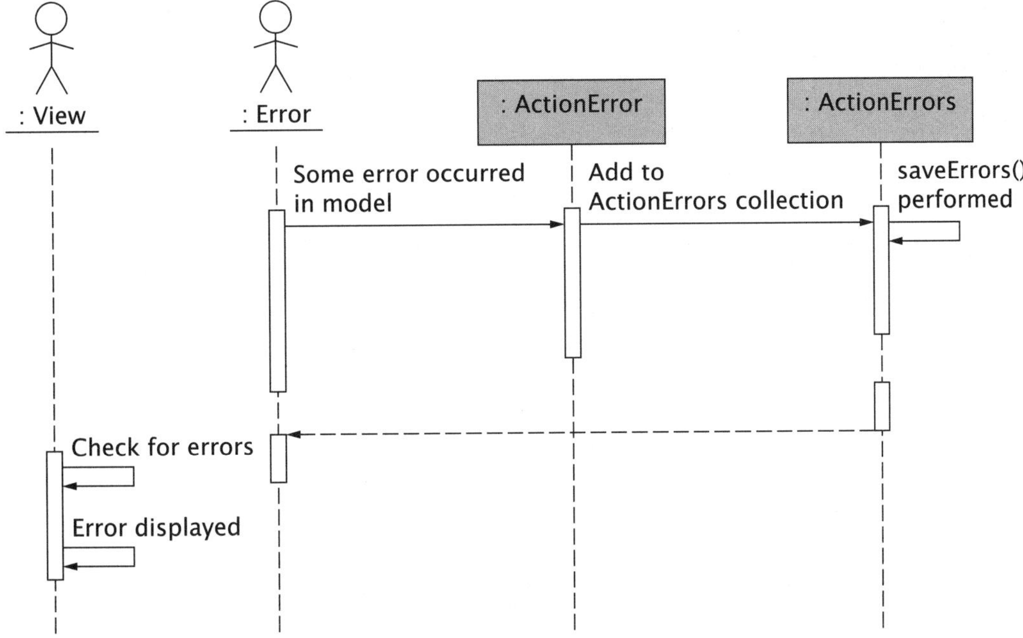


**Figure 4.1:** Error-handling sequence diagram.

## 4.4.2 Declarative Exception Handling

Another approach is to have the Actions themselves delegate exception handling to the `ActionServlet`. One reason for going this route is so your Actions don't have to think about each and every exception that might be thrown from your business logic. It also allows exceptions to be configured within the `struts-config.xml` file.

There are two ways declarative exception handling is accomplished. One is by configuring `<global-exceptions>` in the `struts-config.xml` file. The other is by using the exception element of `<action>` that describes a mapping of an exception that may occur during Action delegation.

The way that the exceptions are declared is very similar to the way that `<global-forwards>` and `<forwards>` are declared. A `<global-exceptions>` configures the global handling of exceptions thrown by Actions to mappable resources using an application-relative URI path. This can be a specific page designed to handle this exception. It is also possible to override an exception handler declared in the global setting by using the exception element in the Action that uses the same type attribute as defined in the global setting.

You can specify the `className` attribute that indicates the implementation subclass of the standard configuration Bean. The default class is

```
org.apache.struts.config.ExceptionConfig
```

The handler attribute is the fully qualified Java class name of the exception handler that should handle this exception. The default is org.apache.struts.action.ExceptionHandler. The key attribute is the message resources key specifying the error message associated with this exception. This is helpful in keeping your errors friendly when your application is internationalized.

The path attribute is the application-relative path of the resource to forward to if this exception occurs. The scope attribute can be set to either "request" or "session" and indicates where the ActionError will be made available. Last but not least is the type attribute. This is the fully qualified Java class name of the exception to be handled. Here's a sample.

In the struts-config.xml, we first declare our <global-exceptions> in the following format:

```
<global-exceptions>
    <exception key="error.required" type="org.apache.struts.util.AppException"
               path="/appError.jsp"/>
</global-exceptions>
```

Here we are declaring that any Action (or business logic) that throws the AppException will be sent to the appError.jsp. We are associating the error.required message string from our ApplicationResource file with this exception. The ApplicationResource file is discussed in detail in Chapter 9 when we talk about internationalization. If you view the mainMenu.jsp of our sample application, there is a link to force an application exception. This makes it easier for you to quickly force an error exception and to follow the flow in the ForceErrorAction.java file. You can add as many <exception> elements to the <global-exceptions> as you like.

Next, we'll look at a specific Action exception declaration.

```
<action   path="/insert"
   ...
 <exception
          key="error.required"
          type="cdmanager.exceptions.MissingValueException"
          path="/insertError.jsp"/>
</action>
```

In this case, we are declaring that if the InsertAction (or business logic that is used by the InsertAction) throws the application-specific exception MissingValueException, then send the exception to the insertError.jsp. Note that in this example, we have defined a specific application exception. This is helpful if you want to wrap other exceptions that might not be as useful to the user in helping him or her understand the problem displayed. For example, you might want to catch SQLExceptions and rethrow them as application-specific exceptions with a more meaningful message to the user.

It is also worth pointing out that matching exceptions to exception handlers takes inheritance into account (i.e., you can declare a handler for a superclass and handle all the exceptions for subclasses of that exception class as well). The matching algorithm works identically to the one used by the servlet container to select <error-page> matches for exceptions.

## 4.5 Handling Tokens

Frequently, in web applications some type of data is submitted and acted upon in the application. A common problem is a user submitting data more than once. This can occur because the user pressed the browser back button, pressed a submit button twice, or even had a bookmark. There must be a way to determine that the request is a duplicate, and so there is. It's done by using tokens. Remember, though, that data entry forms don't always need to use tokens. If the form is written so that there is no state information in the session (i.e., all the data is on the form), you can elect to let the user use the back button. But there are times, even if there is no state information stored in the form, that you still might want to suppress multiple submits. It really depends on the needs of your application. Applying the Synchronizer (or déjà vu) Token pattern is a strategy for addressing the problem of duplicate form submissions. Figure 4.2 is a collaboration diagram for token interaction.

The basic idea is that a synchronizer token is set in a user's session and then is included with each form that is returned to the client. When that particular form is submitted by the client, a comparison of the tokens is done in the Action class. The tokens should match the first time the form is submitted. If a subsequent form submission is done, then the tokens will not match and the submission is not allowed. This is what prevents the user from hitting the browser back button and resubmitting the form. If the tokens do match, then that indicates that things are in sync and a new `Token` is set in the session.[3] Let's look at how to work with Tokens in Action classes.

There is a method provided in the Action class called `isTokenValid()`. The tricky part when dealing with `isTokenValid()` is that the `Token` must exist in two different places, under

[3] For further information on this pattern, see *Core J2EE Patterns—Best Practices and Design Strategies* by Alur, Crupi, and Malks.

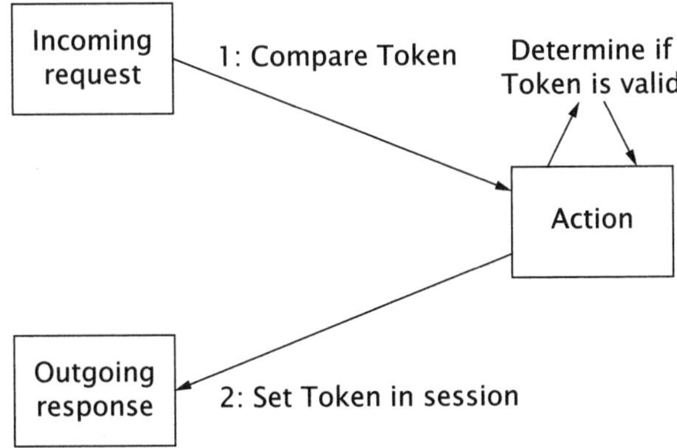


**Figure 4.2:** Token collaboration diagram.

two different keys, in order for the call to return true. The Token must exist in the session with a key of Action.TRANSACTION_TOKEN_KEY, and in the request (as a parameter, not an attribute) with the key of org.apache.struts.taglib.html.Constants.TOKEN_KEY.

A call to saveToken() only puts the Token in the session. It gets put in the request as a hidden form field by the Struts <html:form> tag if the Token is found in the session. Because it is not possible to add a request parameter from inside an Action, the Token is not immediately useful for controlling the flow between Actions during the same request. It is useful for controlling the flow between user requests and Actions.

For example, you may have a page and corresponding action that allows a user to insert a new CD into our CD Manager. The action code may look like this.

```
// Check for a valid token
if(isTokenValid(request)){
        // If the token is value, reset it and perform the business logic
         resetToken(request);
         insertCd(request);
         return mapping.findForward(Globals.FORWARD_SUCCESS);
  }
  else{
        // If not valid, save a new token and forward appropriately
         saveToken(request);
         return mapping.findForward(Globals.FORWARD_INSERT);
  }
```

If the Token is not found in the request, the request will go through the else block, a Token will be saved, and the user will be directed to the appropriate page for inputting new data about the CD. Assuming a Struts <html:form> tag is used on that page, the Token will be added appropriately to the request. When the form is submitted, the request goes through the if block and creates the CD. By resetting the Token here, we ensure that if the user clicks back and tries to resubmit the form, the CD will not be re-created.

## 4.6 Design Rules of Thumb

We've covered a lot of ground so far in terms of Action classes, and there's more. There are some general design issues to remember when coding Action classes. Let's take a look at them.

- Keep scalability in mind. Your Actions should not hold onto scarce resources (e.g., a database connection) across requests. These types of resources should be released prior to forwarding control to the View component. It is good practice to have finally clauses that do these resource releases just in case your Model Bean throws an exception.[4]

---

[4] Finally clauses are used as part of try/catch blocks. A finally clause is always executed regardless of whether you execute your try or catch block code. It is good coding practice to use finally clauses so that you don't accidentally leave resources, like database connections or files open.

- Try to refrain from Action class bloat. Keep your Actions as thin as possible by keeping your business logic in separate Beans. Once you start embedding business logic in your Action, it will continue to grow (sort of like what happens when you try to eat only one Oreo cookie). Once logic is embedded in the Action class, it becomes harder to understand and maintain—not to mention the fact that your code reuse is going down the tubes.
- Remember not to use instance variables in your Actions. If you get the impression that I'm trying to bang this phrase into your head, you are correct. It's fine to have several local methods as long as any properties needed are passed in the method signatures. The JVM handles such properties using the stack, and so they are thread-safe.
- Try to avoid having to write custom Action classes. Using an approach where there is a set of standard Actions that can act upon a known object type or interface drastically reduces the number of custom Actions that must be written. A parameter containing the type of Bean you should create can be passed to the standard Action using the parameter property in the Action configuration. For example,

```
<action
   path="/InsertCD"
   type="cdmanager.actions.CdHelper" <-- standard action -->
   name="insertForm"
   scope="request"
   validate="false"
   parameter="cdmanager.actions.Insert"> <-- specific business bean -->
   <forward name="success"  path="/InsertConf.jsp"/>
 </action>
```

Following this approach makes it possible to write applications that hardly use any custom Actions and allows for the business logic to reside in the business Bean where it belongs.

Another practice worth mentioning, however obvious this might be, is how to name your Action classes. I always find it best to name Actions by what they do rather than by what mapping calls them. The reason for this is simple. If you name your Action class by its purpose, then you can reuse Actions in different mappings. So when you get up to writing complex applications that have lots and lots of Actions, your Action names will not be confusing to other developers. Examples of this are InsertAction, LogonAction, LogoffAction, etc.

## 4.7 Summary

Action classes play an important role in the Struts architecture. We discussed what they are, how to create them, how to structure the execute method, and how to handle exceptions. We also presented a common use of Tokens and covered some basic design strategies when using Actions. Now we turn our attention to the steps necessary to create and build our `ActionForms`.

chapter 5

# Creating and Building ActionForms

This chapter walks through the creation of Struts ActionForms and Dynamic ActionForms, also known as DynaActionForms. The ActionForm Bean is considered part of the View in the MVC model. While it's frequently found that some of the properties in an ActionForm correspond to properties in the Model, the ActionForm is used by the JSP to transfer the state between the View and the Model components. This transfer of information is accomplished by the ActionServlet. Within the process() method of a class used by the ActionServlet called RequestProcessor, the instance of the ActionForm related to the Action we are processing is populated with the appropriate information from the request parameters in the incoming request. In this chapter, we also examine how to build and use these ActionForms.

In general, you create your own ActionForm Bean class by extending org.apache.struts.action.ActionForm. There is typically an ActionForm Bean defined for each of the input forms in your application; however, the implementation is flexible to your application needs. You can have either fine-grained or coarse-grained ActionForm Beans. Fine-grained objects are those that exist where there is a separate ActionForm Bean for every input form. Coarse-grained objects indicate that one Bean handles multiple forms. In theory, you can have one ActionForm for your entire application, but it's not something I recommend unless you have a very simple application that has only one or two input forms in the first place. I suspect that since you are using Struts, your application is a bit more complicated than that.

ActionForms are serializable. In Struts 1.0.2, this was not the case. There were two nonserializable instance variables (servlet and multipartRequestHandler) that were made transient to enable serialization. Explicitly making something transient by using the transient keyword modifier indicates that a field is not part of an object's persistent state. Keep in mind that if you do serialize and deserialize such instances of your ActionForm, these two properties must be explicitly reset, or you might get unexpected and unwanted results.

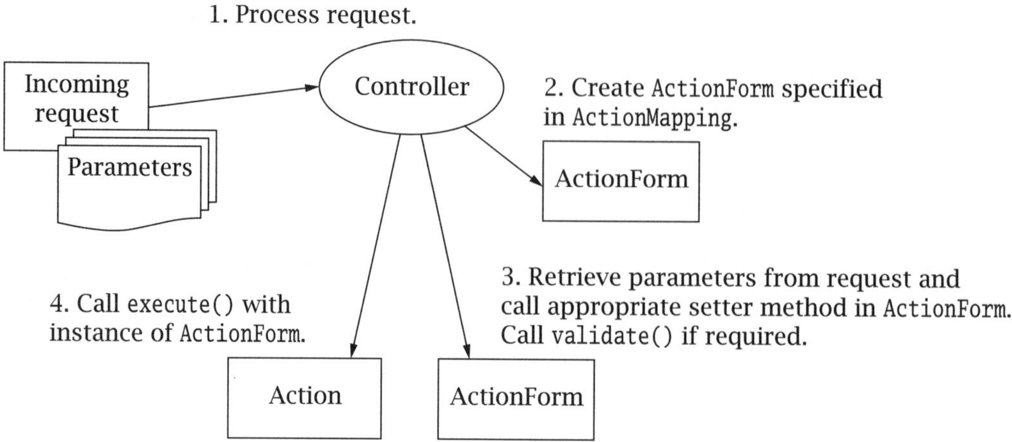


**Figure 5.1:** ActionForm population.

## 5.1 Defining ActionForms

ActionForm Beans are defined in the struts-config.xml file like so:

```
<form-beans>
  <form-bean  name="searchForm" type="cdmanager.forms.SearchForm"/>
</form-beans>
```

You typically have multiple <form-bean> definitions. The name attribute indicates the logical name of the form to be used by Actions. The type attribute is the relative path of the class that will be instantiated when the ActionForm is created.

As a JavaBean, an ActionForm will have only property getter and property setter methods for input fields contained on a form. There is no business logic contained in an ActionForm. One of the main features of the ActionForm is to perform validation prior to the Action's execute() method being called. Figure 5.1 gives an overview of how the request information actually makes it into the ActionForm. Take a look and then we'll examine the steps involved in more detail.

The ActionServlet takes the following steps:

First, the ActionServlet checks the user's session to see if an instance of the ActionForm already exists. A new Bean will be created if none exists, and the new Bean will be added to the user's session.

To determine if the Bean already exists, a lookup is performed using the appropriate key. Using the attribute property in an ActionMapping specifies the key. The attribute is the name of the request scope or session scope attribute under which our form Bean is accessed. This is used if the attribute is something other than the Bean's specified name. Let's look at a simple code example to demonstrate.

```
<action-mappings>
 <action    path="/search"
```

```
            type="cdmanager.actions.SearchAction"
            name="searchForm"
            attribute="myForm"
            scope="request"
            input="/search.jsp">
        <forward name="success" path="/display.jsp"/>
      </action>
    </action-mappings>
```

In this case, the ActionForm is created by looking up the logical name as defined in the form Bean definitions using the name property searchForm. The instance of the class is saved in the session or request (depending on the scope) under the myForm key.

The next step is that the request parameters are examined. For each request parameter that has a corresponding named property in the Bean, the setter method is called. This is accomplished using a combination of RequestUtils, found in the org.apache.struts.util package, and BeanUtils, found in the Jakarta Commons project in the org.apache.commons.beanutils package. The BeanUtils class used to be part of the Struts project, but because of its usefulness to other projects, it has been moved to the Commons project. The BeanUtils provides an easy-to-use wrapper around the more complicated Reflection and Introspection Java APIs.

The corresponding name must be an exact match, case and all. What this translates to is that the names specified as your form fields in your input forms must be declared the same as those in your ActionForm properties. If you find that you have a form field that isn't being populated, first check that the name in your form matches that in your ActionForm class. For those who are familiar with JSP technology, this automatic property population acts the same way as if you used <jsp:setProperty properties="*"/>. If you need more detail about how the setProperty works, see Section 4.2 in the JSP 1.2 specification.

If the validation is turned on once the properties are set, then the validate() method of the ActionForm is called. The validate() method is used to validate any necessary fields prior to the Action's execute() method being called by the ActionServlet. Think of the validate() method as a barrier between your form and its action. If the validation fails, then the request never makes it to the Action for processing. If the validation succeeds, then the updated ActionForm Bean is passed as a parameter to the appropriate Action class in the execute() method signature. The Action class can then pull out whatever information is necessary from the ActionForm.

```
public ActionForward execute(ActionMapping mapping,
                ActionForm form,
                HttpServletRequest request,
                HttpServletResponse response)
        throws Exception {

        String title = ((SearchForm) form).getTitle();
        String artist = ((SearchForm) form).getArtist();
        ...
}
```

## 5.2 ActionForm validate() method

The `validate()` method is used by the `ActionForm` to perform any required validation on input fields that have been submitted. Whether or not the `validate()` method is called is determined by what is specified in the `ActionMapping` definition. When the `validate` property is set to "true," then the `validate()` method of the `ActionForm` will be called by the `ActionServlet`. If `validate` is not specified, then the `execute()` method of the Action class is called. The `validate` property is specified as shown in this action snippet taken from the `struts-config.xml`.

```
<action   path="/insert"
          type="cdmanager.actions.InsertAction"
          name="insertForm"
          scope="request"
          input="/insert.jsp"
          validate="true">
 <forward name="success"  path="/insertConf.jsp"/>
</action>
```

If validate is set to "true," the appropriate validate method will be called. Two method signatures are available.

```
public ActionErrors validate(ActionMapping mapping,
                             javax.servlet.http.HttpServletRequest request)
```

and

```
public ActionErrors validate(ActionMapping mapping,
                             javax.servlet.ServletRequest request)
```

The first one is used for HTTP requests; the second for non-HTTP requests. Usually, the `HttpServletRequest` version is what you'll be interested in. The parameters provide information on the mapping used to select this `ActionForm` instance and the current request. When the method is called, any validation necessary can be performed. This usually consists of checking for required fields and/or by doing pattern checking for valid data, such as an email address or a phone number. If we look at the `ActionForm` example that corresponds to our Logon screen, the `validate()` method is as follows:

```
public ActionErrors validate(ActionMapping mapping,
                             HttpServletRequest request) {

    ActionErrors errors = new ActionErrors();
    if ((username == null) | |  (username.length() < 1))
        errors.add("username", new ActionError("error.username.required"));
    if ((password == null) | |  (password.length() < 1))
        errors.add("password", new ActionError("error.password.required"));

     return errors;

}
```

Here we are using the HttpServletRequest signature version. First, we create our errors collection to be used for the return Object. An empty collection, or a null value, indicates that no errors have occurred and tells the ActionServlet to call the Action's execute() method. For our Logon screen, we are requiring both a username and a password, so we check for both. If either is missing, we generate an ActionError and set the property in that error to the appropriate field. Upon returning the ActionErrors collection, any errors encountered are displayed next to the appropriate field.

The default implementation of validate() performs no validation and returns null. When you create your ActionForm class, it can be subclassed from ActionForm as shown.

```
public final class InsertForm extends ActionForm { ... }
```

The validate() method must override the default to provide any validation necessary. While it is possible to have an ActionForm base class similar to our Action base class, I haven't found a good enough reason for it. Usually, the validation is specific to a particular form, and it is rarely the case that there is a form field on every form you are dealing with in a web application.

## 5.3 ActionForm reset() Method

In addition to the validate() method in each ActionForm, there is also a reset() method available. The reset() method also comes in two flavors, the HttpServletRequest and the ServletRequest version. Here we have the HttpServletRequest version.

```
public void reset(ActionMapping mapping,
                  javax.servlet.http.HttpServletRequest request)
```

The reset() method is also called by the ActionServlet. The first thing that occurs after the ActionServlet obtains the form instance is that the reset() method is called. The purpose of this is to reset all the Bean properties to their default values. This method is called before the properties (based on the incoming request) are repopulated by the ActionServlet. The default values specified in your Bean can be used to prepopulate a form so that fields appear the way you want them to when the form is displayed to the user. The instance of the form used is determined by the scope property in the action mapping.

```
<action   path="/insert"
          type="cdmanager.actions.InsertAction"
          name="insertForm"
          scope="request"
          input="/insert.jsp"
          validate="true">
 <forward name="success"  path="/insertConf.jsp"/>
</action>
```

Remember that if you have a session scope form instance, you get the same instance if one exists already for that session. The scope of your Bean really is determined by your needs. For example, a form that is a set of criteria used for performing a search might be useful within a session. If your scope is set to "request," then every time you go to the page that has the search criteria, a new ActionForm instance is created. In this case, you want to persist your ActionForm between requests in the same session. To solve this quandary, change the scope from "request" to "session," and the ActionServlet will use the appropriate instance.

```
<action   path="/insert"
          type="cdmanager.actions.InsertAction"
          name="insertForm"
          scope="session"
          input="/insert.jsp"
          validate="true">
  <forward name="success"  path="/insertConf.jsp"/>
</action>
```

A request scope form will cause the form instance to be created per request. Even though this might seem obvious, it's worth mentioning because if you have values that you are expecting to be available and they aren't, you'll need to check your scope settings.

As with the validate() method, the default implementation of reset() doesn't perform any logic. When you create your subclassed ActionForm, you must override this method accordingly. To follow through our LogonForm example, the reset method reads as follows:

```
public void reset(ActionMapping mapping, HttpServletRequest request) {
    this.username = null;
    this.password = null;
}
```

There isn't too much magic required in the reset() method. Just remember to handle all the properties on your form; otherwise, you might have values in your properties that aren't what you expect.

## 5.4 Design Rules of Thumb

There are a couple of design rules that can be used when creating ActionForms. First, remember it isn't mandatory even to have an ActionForm Bean. If there is no user data interaction being displayed in the browser, or you don't need any data validated, there is no need to create an accompanying ActionForm. When the action is dispatched from the ActionServlet, a null value will be passed for the ActionForm parameter.

When creating ActionForm Beans, there should be no business logic involved. The Bean should contain only the getter/setter methods for the properties. These are very simple classes to write. For each input field on a form, there should be an accompanying getXxx() and setXxx() method.

It is not necessary to have a one-to-one relationship between your user forms on a JSP and your ActionForms. It is common to have multiple user forms span over many JSPs. We will walk through a wizard sample in just a moment to demonstrate this.

A wizard scenario is one where the user enters some information and then proceeds to the next step, like in a shopping cart checkout. The preferred way to implement this is to define a single `ActionForm` Bean that contains all the properties for all the fields. It is irrelevant which page the fields are actually displayed on. Using this type of design keeps the application simpler. There will only need to be one Action that can handle the various screen forms. It also makes the application more maintainable. Regardless of how the fields are arranged, changed, or added onto the forms, the `ActionForm` and Action will need to be changed in only one place, if at all. If you have `Boolean` properties in your form Bean, which are typically rendered as checkboxes, you *must* set the corresponding instance variables to false in the `reset()` method. Also, if your form fields reflect non-String objects like `int` or `Date`, the form Bean property should still be a `String`. This is important so that a validation error caused by invalid characters will redisplay what the user actually typed, thus meeting the expectation of being able to fix what was wrong without retyping everything.

## 5.5 Wizards, and We're Not Talking Oz

It is quite common in web applications to have input data that spans multiple pages. I'm sure you have experienced a wizard-like page. A shopping cart checkout, as mentioned, or a registration where you have to enter various data and then click a next button are two good examples. Let's walk through a sample implementation of a wizard structure in Struts, and while we do, keep in mind that there are a number of ways to implement wizards. The sample provided uses one JSP for simplicity's sake, but the following points are worth noting. It's possible to implement wizards as separate JSP files and for longer wizards. Having separate JSPs makes maintenance easier, especially if you need to change the sequences because the business rules change.

If you have separate JSPs, they can all still use the same `ActionForm` by having the appropriate hidden fields. To help avoid strange back-button scenarios, a custom tag designed to perform page number checking can be added to the top of each page that would forward to the appropriate page if necessary.

For instance, it is possible to store the `ActionForm` in the session (which is a simple approach), but it doesn't scale as well doing it this way. And as the session grows, it becomes expensive to maintain. Another reason not to take this approach (depending on how complicated your application server environment is) is that you might have to worry about having multiple application server support for fail-over. It can be argued that the application server will usually provide a mechanism for handling this, but it is a point worth considering. While there are other ways to implement wizards, the way I'll demonstrate is fairly simple and should work for most situations. If you are doing more complicated workflow logic, it probably is worthwhile to check out the Struts workflow extension written by Matthias Bauer that is found at *www.livinglogic.de/Struts/*.

We'll walk through a two-step wizard. You'll get the idea of what needs to be done, and then you can easily expand this to be an $n$-step wizard as your application requires. When allowing for wizard-type functionality, usually you want the user to navigate with a next-previous button layout on the form, not by using the browser back or forward buttons. One of the key reasons for using a wizard structure is the requirement that state must be maintained across pages without the use of the session or other types of persistence, such as storing and retrieving information from a database.

We want to design our wizard so that we use the same JSP and Action class for each step in the process. This is accomplished by using different Struts custom tags, specifically <logic:equal>, to identify which portion of the JSP is of interest. We'll add a wizard to our CD Manager that allows us to enter a title and artist and then complete a review of that CD.

So, we have the following steps:

1. Enter CD title and artist.
2. Complete CD review and submit.

The ActionForm contains the following:

```
public final class WizardForm extends ActionForm {

    private String title = null;
    private String artist = null;
    private String review = null;
    private String currentStep = "1";
    private String action = null;
       ...
       // Respective getters/setters/reset/validate methods
}
```

The title, artist, and review are the various fields that will appear in a particular form. We are only using one ActionForm; therefore all the fields are contained in the WizardForm even if you use multiple JSPs. The currentStep is used to determine which step in the wizard we are processing. The action is used to determine which button has been pushed on the Submit. Since we can have multiple buttons per form (e.g., previous, next, done), we need to be able to distinguish them.

Remember, we want to use a request scope for our ActionForm. By using a request scope, a new ActionForm is created for each request. While there is a slight overhead to creating a new instance each time, it is less than having to pass a loaded session around in an application server. To accomplish the goal of having the ActionForm in request scope, it is important to have all the input fields for each page in the wizard suite included on every page. However, the fields that are not being displayed on the current page will use the Struts <html:hidden> custom tag instead of <html:text> tag, or whatever your input field is. By including the <html:hidden> tag, the ActionForm Bean fields will persist from step to step. This also allows use of the previous-next buttons on the form.

Let's look at the sample components to get the wizard working. In our struts-config.xml file, we configure our required forms and actions as

```
<form-bean name="wizardForm" type="cdmanager.forms.WizardForm"/>
```

First, we define our form Bean. Next we define our action mapping.

```
<action     path="/wizard"
            type="cdmanager.actions.WizardAction"
            name="wizardForm"
            scope="request"
            validate="true"
            input="/wizard.jsp">
  <forward name="next" path="/wizard.jsp"/>
  <forward name="success" path="/wizarddone.jsp"/>
</action>
```

Notice that the scope of the wizardForm is set to "request" causing a new form to be created for each request. We will be using validation on this wizard to demonstrate how to validate only certain fields. The input property defines what JSP should be displayed if an error occurs during validation. We have two forward mappings—one if the next button is pressed, and one that is used when the wizard is completed. The reason we always use wizard.jsp for the "next" forward is we are only working with one JSP file. It is possible to have more than one JSP, and you would handle your forwards accordingly.

Next, let's examine the contents of our JSP and comment on each section. For the complete JSP file, reference the wizard.jsp file contained in the sample application download.

```
<html:form action="/wizard">
```

Our form will be submitted to the wizard action that we just defined in our struts-config.xml. Next, we will use various Struts custom tags (full details on the tags will be discussed in Chapter 8), to determine what step in our wizard we are working on. This is what the currentStep property is used for.

```
<!--
     Set up for step 1
     Note that we set Step 1 as the default in the ActionForms step property
  -->
<logic:equal name="wizardForm" property="currentStep"
          scope="request" value="1">
```

If we are on step 1, then we set our hidden properties accordingly so that they will be set in the new ActionForm that is created for this request. We only set properties to hidden if they will not be displayed on the current page.

```
<html:hidden property="currentStep" value="1"/>
<html:hidden property="review" />
```

Next, we set up the fields that will be visible on this page. We have the artist and title fields, along with the next button. Notice that the property of the <html:submit> is set to "action." This is so we can have a common property for all buttons and simply determine which one was pressed by checking the value. The value is defined using the <bean:message> custom tag so that all of our labels come from the application resource file and can be easily internationalized. When a button is pressed, the action on the form is executed.

```
<table>
    <tr>
           <th align="left"><bean:message key="prompt.artist"/></th>
           <td> <html:text property="artist"
                                size="25" maxlength="25"/><br></td>
    </tr>
    <tr>
    <th align="left"><bean:message key="prompt.title"/></th>
    <td> <html:text property="title"
                         size="25" maxlength="25"/><br></td>
    </tr>
    <tr><td></td><td align="right">
      <html:submit property="action" >
               <bean:message key="button.next"/>
           </html:submit>
           </td>
      </tr>
</table>
</logic:equal>
```

Continuing through our JSP, we have another `<logic:equal>` tag. We use the logic tags to determine which of the fields are to be displayed. If our `currentStep` is set to "2," then we will display the second page in the wizard. We have the various hidden fields that won't be displayed, but we still want to have the information passed to the `WizardForm`.

On the second page of the wizard, we simply display a `textarea` that is used to enter a commentary for the CD review. Notice our submit button still has the property of "action," but the value is not that of the done button. Again, we're just demonstrating a simple two-step wizard; if you had more steps, you would simply use a next-previous button structure and continue to set your `currentStep` accordingly.

```
<!-- Step two -->
<logic:equal name="wizardForm" property="currentStep"
                scope="request" value="2">
                 <html:hidden property="artist" />
     <html:hidden property="title" />
     <html:hidden property="currentStep" value="2" />
<table>
        <tr>
            <th align="left"><bean:message key="prompt.review"/></th>
            <td><html:textarea property="review"
                                rows="10" /><br></td>
     </tr>
     <tr>
     <td align="right">
            <html:submit property="action" >
                  <bean:message key="button.previous"/>
            </html:submit></td>
            <td align="left">
```

```
            <html:submit property="action" >
                <bean:message key="button.done"/>
            </html:submit>
            </td>
        </table>
        </logic:equal>
</html:form>
```

Since we have validation set to "true" in the action mapping that we looked at in our struts-config.xml, let's briefly look at the validation() method. By checking to see what the currentStep is set to, we can determine the fields requiring validation for a particular step.

```
public ActionErrors validate(ActionMapping mapping,
                             HttpServletRequest request) {

    ActionErrors errors = new ActionErrors();
    if (currentStep.equals("1")) {
        if (((title == null) | |  (title.length() < 1)))
            errors.add("title", new ActionError("error.title.required"));
        if(((artist == null)| |  (artist.length() < 1)))
            errors.add("artist", new ActionError("error.artist.required"));
    } else if ((review == null) | |  (review.length() <1)){
            errors.add("review", new ActionError("error.review.required"));
      }
    return errors;
  }
```

When one of the submit buttons is pressed on the displayed page, the WizardAction is called. The code of most interest to us looks like what follows. I'm going to comment on the code section by section.

First, we create our errors collection, and retrieve our form instance that is passed into our execute() method.

```
ActionErrors errors = new ActionErrors();
WizardForm wizardForm = (WizardForm)form;
```

Next we check to see what step in the wizard we are up to and which button was pressed by retrieving the action property value. We retrieve the comparison value using messages.getMessage(), which will look up the key from the ApplicationResource file. This way the comparison will be correct regardless of the locale being used. When the appropriate forward is determined, the ForwardMapping is returned.

```
if (wizardForm.getCurrentStep().equals("1") &&
      (wizardForm.getAction().equals(messages.getMessage("button.next")))){
            wizardForm.setCurrentStep("2");
            return (mapping.findForward("next"));
}
```

```
if (wizardForm.getCurrentStep().equals("2") &&
        (wizardForm.getAction().equals(messages.getMessage("button.done")))){
              return (mapping.findForward(Globals.FORWARD_SUCCESS));
}else {
        wizardForm.setCurrentStep( "1" );
        return (mapping.findForward("next"));
}
```

The key point is that the currentStep is being set to the correct value in the wizardForm and will be set as a hidden value. The <logic:equal> tags in the JSP will use that value to determine which is the correct page to display. In this sample, we have only two forms in the wizard, but it is quite simple to extend this to however many forms you are dealing with.

Using this basic format, you are able to create more complicated wizard functionality that is cleanly implemented.

## 5.6 Other Wizard Variations

While the approach we just talked about should work in most situations, here are a few other ideas that you might find useful.

If you have different actions, for instance, an "insert, update, delete," and you want to associate different validations with each one, you can assign a different property to each submit button.

```
<html:submit property="insertSubmit">
   <bean:message key="button.newRecord"/>
</html:submit>

 <html:submit property="updateSubmit">
     <bean:message key="button.updateRecord"/>
 </html:submit>
```

Then in the ActionForm validate(), retrieve and check the values.

```
boolean doInsert=(request.getParameter("insertSubmit") != null);
boolean doUpdate=(request.getParameter("updateSubmit") != null);
```

And then validate accordingly.

```
 if (doInsert | |  doUpdate) {
        ...do something...
} else if (doDelete){
        ...do something else...
}
```

It is also possible to define forms so that you can use the same form Bean, but use a different name depending on the action. For example,

```
<form-bean name="myAddForm" type="package.MyForm" />
<form-bean name="myUpdateForm" type="package.MyForm" />
<form-bean name="myDeleteForm" type="package.MyForm" />
```

You can use the same form Bean—MyForm—but identify it by different names depending upon the action invoked.

```
<action     path="/some/add"
            type="package.MyAction"
            scope="request"
            name="myAddForm"
            validate="true"
            input="/add.jsp"
            parameter="Add">
</action>
```

As you can see, there are a variety of ways to address this problem. The correct implementation for you depends on the needs of your application.

## 5.7 DynaActionForms

Now that you have a clear understanding of what can be done with ActionForms, let's add one more type to the mix. DynaActionForms provide a convenient mechanism that eliminates the need to write ActionForms at all. DynaActionForm, introduced in Struts 1.1, allows for properties to be dynamic. What this means is that you can define properties in your struts-config.xml file and use the type of the form to be org.apache.struts.action.DynaActionForm. Nothing more needs to be written. DynaActionForms accomplish this by making use of the DynaBean provided in the Apache Commons project. This dynamic behavior is provided through reflection and HashMaps. You can look at the following classes:

- org.apache.commons.beanutils.ConversionException
- org.apache.commons.beanutils.DynaBean
- org.apache.commons.beanutils.DynaClass
- org.apache.commons.beanutils.DynaProperty

It is a bit beyond the scope of this book to go into the DynaBean internals in the Apache Commons project, but if you have a burning desire to peek at the internals, you can go right ahead.

A DynaActionForm is defined in the struts-config.xml using the <form-bean> and <form-property> elements as follows:

```
<form-bean      name="insertDynaForm"
                type="org.apache.struts.action.DynaActionForm">
  <form-property name="artist" type="java.lang.String"/>
  <form-property name="title" type="java.lang.String"/>
  <form-property name="genre" initial="Dance" type="java.lang.String"/>
</form-bean>
```

The attributes of a dynamic form are similar to those of a standard ActionForm. The name is used to reference this form Bean in Actions, and the type specifies the class to be instantiated. When using the DynaActionForm class, the dynamic attribute of the <form-bean> automatically defaults to “true.” For a DynaActionForm, you specify all the properties of the form by using the <form-property> element. The name is the property name. The type is the fully qualified Java class name of the implementation class of this Bean property. If this is an indexed property, you can follow the type by []. You'll notice that in the last <form-property> defining the genre property, we are setting the initial (or default) value to be “Dance.” This is the value that is also used when the reset() method is called on a DynaActionForm. If nothing is specified in the initial attribute, then all primitive types are set to zero, while objects are set to null.

It can be very convenient to use DynaActionForm. One of the main advantages is that you have to write less code. Nothing other than what we just defined in the code sample is required to use the form just as we use any other form. The one issue to be aware of is validation. When using DynaActionForm, there is an assumption that validation is handled someplace other than the ActionForm. It is possible to implement validation within your Action itself, but there is a better approach.

To do validation, you can use the DynaValidatorForm, or DynaValidatorActionForm, both found in the org.apache.struts.validator package. By extending the DynaActionForm, basic field validation can be provided based on an XML file. Validation is based on the key passed into the validator. This key is the name attribute from the struts-config.xml file. This should match the form element's name attribute in the validation.xml. We talk more about the ValidatorPlugin and validation.xml in Chapter 9 when we discuss other useful Struts packages. Another option is to subclass DynaActionForm and just write a validate() method. You don't need to write all the getters and setters. This approach is also useful if you just need a custom reset() method.

It is clearly simpler to create a DynaActionForm, and therefore maintenance of your application becomes easier.

## 5.8 Summary

This chapter demonstrated what ActionForms and DynaActionForms are and how to use them. It looked at some basic design strategies, and it took us on a walkthrough of how to build wizard functionality forms. It should be obvious that there is a close tie between ActionForms and how the custom tags work in conjunction with the forms. We'll be taking closer look at the details of the custom tags in Chapter 8.

chapter 6

# Configuring Struts

Previous chapters covered how to create and build your Actions and ActionForms and touched base on the `ActionServlet`. This chapter details how to configure those Actions, the ActionForms, and the `ActionServlet` instance. It also discusses the two primary configuration files: `struts-config.xml` and `web.xml`. You'll notice the XML extension on those files. This chapter assumes a basic understanding of how to read XML files as discussed in Chapter 1. If you need to come up to speed on working with XML files, see *www.w3schools.com/xml/default.asp* for a quick tutorial.

## 6.1 Web.xml

We start with the web application deployment descriptor, also called the `web.xml` file. Before being able to use Struts, you must set up your JSP container so that it knows to map all appropriate requests with a certain file extension to the Struts `ActionServlet` instance. The Servlet specification includes a Document Type Descriptor (DTD) for the web application deployment descriptor. The elements in `web.xml` must match the order defined in the DTD, but not all containers enforce this requirement. For maximum portability, be sure your elements are in the correct positions. If you are interested in reading through the entire Servlet 2.3 specification, you can find it at *jcp.org/aboutJava/communityprocess/first/jsr053/servlet23_PFD.pdf*. The `web.xml` is found in the `WEB-INF` directory of your web application. It describes everything that the server needs to know about your application except the context path for the application. This makes sense because if the `web.xml` defined the context path, you'd be in a chicken-and-egg situation. The context path is defined by the system administrator when an application is deployed in a particular web or application server. Depending on your web or app server, this is done in different ways, and you should check the documentation for the particular server you are using. Setup instructions for some of the more popular application servers have been included on the Struts site at *jakarta.apache.org/struts/*. Just click on the installation link to find the server you are interested in.

Information included in the web.xml includes the servlets and other components that make up an application, init parameters, mappings, and container-managed security constraints. The web.xml file is read when the JSP container starts. As it relates to Struts, the web.xml is a standard file, so regardless of which JSP container (or web application server) you are using, the Struts-specific pieces should still apply.

The vanilla version of the ActionServlet controller (i.e., the one you use if you aren't overriding any of the ActionServlet methods) has a number of supported initialization parameters that can be specified in the web.xml. If you subclass the ActionServlet to address any special behavior that you require, additional initialization parameters can be defined and accessed. The values actually assigned to these initialization parameters can be retrieved in a servlet or JSP by calling

```
String value = getServletContext().getInitParameter("name");
```

where "name" matches the <param-name> element of one of these initialization parameters. Using application-specific initialization parameters in your web.xml is a way to change the deployment parameters of your application without having to redeploy the entire application.

Let's walk through the web.xml for the CD Manager application. I am showing an abbreviated version here in the text. If you want the full web.xml version with all comments, access it in the WEB-INF directory of the download that accompanies this book. Lines beginning with <!-- are XML comments.

```
<web-app>
    <display-name>Struts CD Manager Sample Application</display-name>
    <description>
       This is the 1.0 version of the sample application
       used in the book The Struts Framework: Practical Guide for Java
       Programmers  (MK 2003)
    </description>
```

First, we define our web app using the <web-app> element. The <display-name> and <description> are optional, but informative. Next, we define our Servlet by using the <servlet> element. The <servlet-name> defines the canonical name that the Servlet is referenced by. The <servlet-class> defines the fully qualified class name of the class used to instantiate this Servlet.

```
<servlet>
    <servlet-name>cdmanager</servlet-name>
    <servlet-class>org.apache.struts.action.ActionServlet</servlet-class>
```

## 6.1.1 Using Subapplications

Any initialization parameters are then defined using the <init-param> element. It is possible in Struts 1.1 to have multiple subapplications defined and supported. What this means is that you can break your application into various subapplications for better maintenance. You no longer have to camp outside the person's cubicle who has the one and only struts-config.xml file checked out of source control.

Another reason to consider using subapplications is for control flow that varies by client. In some applications, you may have a standard set of pages, but the control flow may vary depending on what client logs into the application. You could store this control flow meta-data into a database and generate the `web.xml` (or portions thereof) file along with all the various `struts-config.xml` files.

If you have ever worked with Struts 1.x, you probably noticed that many of the elements defined in the `web.xml` file have been moved to the `struts-config.xml` in Struts 1.1. This is because they are now application specific. Multiple subapplications are identified by a prefix at the beginning of the context-relative portion of the request URI. If no application prefix can be matched, the default configuration is selected. The default has a prefix equal to a zero-length string. Implementing the default this way allows for backward compatibility with Struts 1.0.x where it was possible to have only one application defined.

We are using only one application in our CD Manager application because it is relatively small in scope. If you had a large-scale application that contained different functional areas, then it would make sense to consider having subapplications that work together instead of one big application. If we were to break our sample application into subapplications, those subapps would be defined using the following elements in the `web.xml` file:

```
<!-- The default subapplication -->
<init-param>
  <param-name>config</param-name>
  <param-value>/WEB-INF/struts-config.xml</param-value>
</init-param>

<!-- The catalog subapplication -->
<init-param>
  <!-- catalog prefix -->
  <param-name>config/catalog</param-name>
  <param-value>/WEB-INF/struts-config-catalog.xml</param-value>
</init-param>

<!-- The sorter subapplication -->
<init-param>
  <!-sorter prefix -->
  <param-name>config/sorter</param-name>
  <param-value>/WEB-INF/struts-config-sorter.xml</param-value>
</init-param>
```

When using subapplications, you might define the context-relative request URIs to specify which subapp to use. For example, the action on a form might appear as

```
<html:form action="/logon" >
```

which refers to the default subapplication or

```
<html:form action="/catalog/listCds" >
```

which refers to the Action class in the catalog subapplication. You don't actually have to do this. You can use "/listCds" if you want within the catalog subapplication. The basic rule is this: all `struts-config.xml` parameters that were *context* relative in 1.0 are now *subapp-prefix* relative in 1.1. That way, a single application can be used either as the default subapplication or as a named subapplication with no change.

Note that when using a multiple subapp environment, there is still a single instance of the controller Servlet. However, there can be multiple `struts-config.xml` files—one per subapplication—as was shown earlier. The information contained in the specific `struts-config.xml` is the information stored in each `ApplicationConfig` object.

In order for this subapp feature to work, any request for a presentation page that uses elements from the configuration file, including ActionForms, Forwards, and ActionMappings, must be routed through the controller. This allows the controller to make the appropriate configuration available for a given page. The controller Servlet in 1.1 now creates two request attributes for all requests that flow through the controller so that configurations specific to that subapplication can be identified. These request attributes are `Action.APPLICATION_KEY`, which contains the `ApplicationConfig` instance for the subapplication selected by the current request URI, and `Action.MESSAGES_KEY`, which contains the `MessageResources` instance for the subapplication selected by the current request URI. Both of these String constants are defined in the Action class and are used as the key to look up the request attributes.

In order for both of the request attributes to be set, all requests must pass through the controller. Having requests pass through the controller is not new to Struts 1.1. While it might have been possible to bypass this by having direct linking to pages, it is good design practice to make sure everything flows through the controller. If we think back to our MVC model, this is the way it should be anyway. Many other features in advanced applications, including security and logging, are easier to implement when everything passes through the controller.[1]

### 6.1.2 Other Initialization Parameters

As we continue through our `web.xml` file, there are also various debugging parameters specifying the debug level and the detail that should be displayed. The validate parameter is used to specify whether a validating XML parser should be used to read the configuration file.

```
<init-param>
  <param-name>debug</param-name>
  <param-value>2</param-value>
</init-param>
<init-param>
  <param-name>detail</param-name>
  <param-value>2</param-value>
```

---

[1] In the 20%, but still-worth-pointing-out category, requests in a subapp are assumed to go back to that subapp. Switching from one subapp to another can be accomplished programmatically, via `RequestUtils.selectApplication()`, or through a hyperlink using the new standard action `SwitchAction`.

```
</init-param>2
<init-param>
  <param-name>validate</param-name>
  <param-value>true</param-value>
</init-param>
```

The <load-on-startup> parameter comes from the Servlet specification and tells the server what the preference order to load this Servlet is when the application starts. If a positive integer is specified, then it will be used to determine the load order. Lower values are loaded first. If there is no value, or if the value is a negative number, then the container is free to load the servlets in any order during startup.

```
<load-on-startup>2</load-on-startup>
```

Then we complete our Servlet element with </servlet>.

### 6.1.3 Defining the Servlet Mapping

The Servlet mapping element defines the mapping between a Servlet and a URL pattern. The <servlet-name> specifies the Servlet we are associating with a given URL pattern. This should match the <servlet-name> used when defining the Servlet in the <servlet> element. The URL pattern is specified by using the <url-pattern> element.

```
<!-- Action Servlet Mapping -->
  <servlet-mapping>
    <servlet-name>cdmanager</servlet-name>
    <url-pattern>*.do</url-pattern>
  </servlet-mapping>
```

It is common practice to use the .do extension for action classes; however, nothing prevents you from defining whatever extension you want as long as it follows the syntax rules. As defined in the Servlet 2.3 specification, the following syntax is used to define mappings:

- A string beginning with a / character and ending with a /* postfix is used as a path mapping.
- A string beginning with a *. prefix is used as an extension mapping.
- All other strings are used as exact matches only.
- A string containing only the / character indicates that servlet specified by the mapping becomes the "default" servlet of the application. In this case, the servlet path is the request URI minus the context path, and the path info is null.

[2]The "debug" and "detail" parameters are deprecated in 1.1, which uses commons-logging instead of the built-in logging code in 1.0.

**Table 6.1:** Servlet mapping examples.

| Sample | Request path | Servlet |
|---|---|---|
| 1 | /logon.do | cdmanager1 |
| 2 | /bar/logon.do | cdmanager1 |
| 3 | /foo/bar/logon.html | cdmanager2 |
| 4 | /bar | cdmanager3 |
| 5 | /bar/logon.html | Default servlet |

This makes more sense by using a sample. Let's say we have three servlet mappings that specify three different servlets.

```
<!-- Action Servlet Mapping -->
  <servlet-mapping>
    <servlet-name>cdmanager1</servlet-name>
    <url-pattern>*.do</url-pattern>
  </servlet-mapping>
  <servlet-mapping>
    <servlet-name>cdmanager2</servlet-name>
    <url-pattern>/foo/*</url-pattern>
  </servlet-mapping>
  <servlet-mapping>
    <servlet-name>cdmanager3</servlet-name>
    <url-pattern>/bar</url-pattern>
  </servlet-mapping>
```

In this case, the incoming path requests shown in Table 6.1 would result in the specified Servlet handling the request.

In Sample 1, /logon.do matches the *.do URL-pattern, so the request will be routed to cdmanager1. In Sample 2, /bar/logon.do also matches the *.do pattern. The reason that we don't use the URL-pattern /bar is there is no * specified, so it will only match the exact URL /bar. Sample 3 matches our /foo/* pattern, so the request will be sent to cdmanager2. Note that when * is specified, it matches everything after the prefix.

Sample 4 is an exact match of our /bar URL-pattern and is sent to cdmanager3. Sample 5 falls through all the URL-patterns because we don't have *.html specified in any of the definitions. Therefore, it will be sent to the Servlet that is the default for the server. For Struts, the only two practical URL-patterns are path matching (/foo/*) and extension mapping (*.do). In addition, you must use extension matching if you are using subapplications.

### 6.1.4 The Welcome File List

The <welcome-file-list> contains an ordered list of welcome file elements. The <welcome-file> element contains the filename to use as a default welcome file, such as index.jsp in our case.

```
<!-- The Welcome File List -->
  <welcome-file-list>
    <welcome-file>index.jsp</welcome-file>
  </welcome-file-list>
```

Note, though, that the welcome file list defines the default file(s) for all directories, including the root and all subdirectories. It does not specify the URL of a default page for the web application. So if you request *testserver/app/*, the application looks for *testserver/app/index.jsp*. If you request *testserver/app/mydirectory/*, the application looks for *testserver/app/mydirectory/index.jsp*. It's a subtle point, but one worth mentioning.

### 6.1.5 Defining the Custom Tag Libraries

It is possible to utilize custom tag libraries in your web application. A number of custom tag libraries are used in the Struts framework. If you define your own custom tag libraries, they must follow the same syntax. When defining a tag library, the `<taglib>` element is used to describe the JSP tag library. It contains two elements. The first is the `<taglib-uri>` that describes a URI, relative to the location of the `web.xml` file and identifies a tag library that is used in the web application.

The second is the `<taglib-location>` that contains the location of the tag library descriptor (TLD) file that defines the tags used in this library. The location is defined as a resource relative to the root of the web application.

In our sample application, we also have a tag library that we defined ourselves called `app.tld`. It's not uncommon to have the `<taglib-uri>` and the `<taglib-location>` be the same place. Even though it is defined the same way, this is a sample using one of the Struts TLD files. For the full taglib listing, refer to the `web.xml` file in the sample application download. We will be talking about the taglibs in more detail in the next chapter.

```
<taglib>
  <taglib-uri>/WEB-INF/app.tld</taglib-uri>
  <taglib-location>/WEB-INF/app.tld</taglib-location>
</taglib>

<!-- Struts Tag Library Descriptors -->
<taglib>
  <taglib-uri>/WEB-INF/struts-bean.tld</taglib-uri>
  <taglib-location>/WEB-INF/struts-bean.tld</taglib-location>
</taglib>
```

By defining the tag libraries available to our application in the `web.xml`, we are able to reference them in a JSP file.

```
<%@ taglib uri="/WEB-INF/struts-bean.tld" prefix="bean" %>
```

Once the library is declared in the JSP, the tags available in the library may be accessed and used by referring to the prefix of the library. A sample access of the message tag provided in the `struts-bean.tld` looks like `<bean:message key="prompt.password"/>` in the JSP file.

### 6.1.6 Other Elements

There are other elements available in the web.xml that can be specified for security, security roles, error-handling, data, or EJB configuration, to name a few of the elements. However, to go into all the available elements in the web.xml is a bit beyond the scope here. We've hit upon the basic elements required to configure and use a web.xml document with Struts. If you are interested in the other types of elements available for advanced applications, see Chapter 13 of the Servlet 2.3 specification found at *jcp.org/aboutJava/communityprocess/first/jsr053/servlet23_PFD.pdf*.

## 6.2 Struts-config.xml

Once we have our JSP/Servlet container configured using the web.xml, our attention turns to the struts-config.xml file used for defining the Struts-specific aspects of your application. The struts-config.xml file can be used to define areas that include

- Data sources
- Form Bean definitions
- Global exceptions
- Global forwards
- Action mappings
- Controller configuration

We've already talked about the global exceptions and gone through an example. Let's look at each of the others in more detail.

### 6.2.1 Defining Data Sources

If you need to define data sources for your application, you can by using the <data-sources> element and then defining each data source using the <data-source> element and various attributes. In our sample application, I am using MySql and the associated MySql JDBC driver. MySql is a popular open source database and can be found at *www.mysql.com*.

```
<data-sources>
    <data-source
     autoCommit="false"
     description="CD Manager sample datasource"
     driverClass="org.gjt.mm.mysql.Driver"
     maxCount="4"
     minCount="2"
     password="mysql"
     url="jdbc:mysql://localhost/cdsample"
     user="developer"/>
</data-sources>
```

It is then possible to access the data source from an Action class by using the following line of code:

```
DataSource dataSource =
(DataSource)servlet.getServletContext().getAttribute(Action.DATA_SOURCE_KEY);
```

The Action.DATA_SOURCE_KEY is a String constant defined as org.apache.struts.action.DATA_SOURCE in the Action class and is used to reference the context attribute key under which the default configured data source is stored. This attribute will be set if a data source is configured for this application. When you are using data sources, make sure that your attributes, like the user and password, are set correctly for your data source access. When the Struts controller (ActionServlet) initializes, it tries to initialize the defined data sources as well. If there is a problem with initialization, the ActionServlet init fails, but it might not be obvious why it failed. Look in the server logs for the exact error message. When using Tomcat 4.x, this would be the $CATALINA.HOME/logs directory.

### 6.2.2 Defining Form Beans

Form Bean definitions are used to describe configuration of the ActionForms used in Struts. Defining form Beans is simple. All form Beans are contained within the <form-beans> element. Each form Bean is defined by specifying the logical name of the form and the type of class it is. The name is what is used by the action mappings. The type is simply the fully qualified classname of your ActionForm class. The following sample shows some of the forms available in the CD Manager application:

```
<form-beans>
  <form-bean      name="logonForm"
                  type="cdmanager.forms.LogonForm"/>
  <form-bean      name="searchForm"
                  type="cdmanager.forms.SearchForm"/>
</form-beans>
```

### 6.2.3 Defining Global Forwards

Global forwards are just that; they are global definitions that can be referenced from your action classes or JSP files without having an explicit forward definition defined in your action mapping. Think of global forwards as "includes" to your action mappings. They are available to all actions in the application that require a forward. The advantage of using a global forward is that by having everything located in your struts-config.xml file, if changes must be made in your application, they must be done in only one place. A sample of a <global-forwards> definition is

```
<global-forwards>
  <forward   name="logoff"  path="/logoff.do"/>
  <forward   name="logon"   path="/logon.jsp"/>
</global-forwards>
```

Each <forward> defines the canonical name that the forward will be referenced by and the path that should be forwarded to. Notice that you can have both actions and direct pages specified. There is also a redirect attribute that can be set to "true" or "false" depending on if you want a redirect performed or not.

```
<forward  name="logon"  path="/logon.jsp" redirect="true"/>
```

***Forwards vs. Redirects.*** So how do you decide when you want to forward and when you want to redirect? It depends on the needs of your application, but there are a couple of important differences to consider that can help you decide. When you forward, the target page is invoked by the JSP container through an internal method call on the server. Therefore, the same request is used for the processing on the new page and the browser is none the wiser (i.e., you still see the original URL on the address line in the browser). When doing a redirect, the page doing the redirect informs the browser to make a new request to the target page. The URL shown in the browser therefore changes to the URL of the new page. When doing a redirect, any request scope objects are no longer available to the new page because the browser creates a new request. If you need the information from the request, you can either pass it as a request parameter or save the data in a session or application scope object.

Most of the time you will be using forwards, but there might be circumstances that require you to use a redirect. In situations where you are using cookies or have pages that update information (e.g., when inserting information into a database), you probably want to use redirect so that on a page reload that action isn't performed again.

## 6.2.4 Defining Action Mappings

The action mappings are used to determine the flow of your application. They are the roadmap for the entire Struts framework. The action mappings tell the controller what classes to instantiate for Actions, what forms to use when calling the execute() method of the Actions, and what forwards are to be used from the execute() method return. Action mappings are straightforward to write. All action mappings are defined within the <action-mappings> element. Each action mapping is defined by an <action> element.

There are two types of action mappings: those that use form Beans and those that don't. Actions that use a form Bean are those that require some type of data input. If no data is required, then the form Bean is omitted and a null is passed to the execute() method of the Action.

Let's look at the wizard action from our sample application. The wizard action is a typical action mapping that requires a form Bean.

```
<action-mappings>
    <action    path="/wizard"
               type="cdmanager.actions.WizardAction"
               name="wizardForm"
               scope="request"
               validate="true"
               input="/wizard.jsp">
      <forward name="next" path="/wizard.jsp"/>
```

```
        <forward name="success" path="/wizarddone.jsp"/>
    </action>
<action-mappings>
```

The path attribute gives the path used to refer to this action. As we've seen from our JSPs, this is what is on the action attribute of a form submission. The type gives the full, context-relative class path to the Action class that should be instantiated for this Action.

The scope attribute defines whether this action should have either request or session scope. The default is session, but you are encouraged to use request scope unless you truly require session scope. Validate indicates whether or not the controller (ActionServlet) should call the validate() method of the ActionForm specified for this action. The input attribute gives the path to the JSP that should be displayed if there is an error or exception that occurs during the ActionForm validation. If you have the validate attribute set to "true," you need to supply an input value; otherwise, you will get a runtime error.

There can be any number of forwards defined in an action mapping and then used by the Action class to return the next page (or action) that is called by the controller. This is where the lookup that we've seen using the return mapping.findForward("success") call in our Action class gets its information. Remember, any global forward definition can also be used as a lookup return value for the Action. For example, we previously defined a global forward to "logon" that will forward to the /login.jsp file. Any Action within our application can do a return mapping.findForward("logon") and will be forwarded to the /login.jsp page. Keep in mind what we mentioned earlier regarding forwards. Local forward definitions for the same logical name will override the global one for that action only.

### 6.2.5 Action Attributes

There are a number of other attributes that can be specified in an <action> element. Let's walk through them.

The attribute attribute (no, that's not a typo) is a request scope or session scope attribute name under which our form Bean is accessed if it is different from the form Bean's name specified in the name attribute. For example, if we have an action defined

```
<action
 path="/insert"
 type=" cdmanager.actions.Insert"
 name="cdForm"
 attribute="newCdForm"
</action>
```

the string "newCdForm" would be used to search the scope for the existence of the form instead of the string "cdForm."

The forward attribute is the context-relative path of the web application resource that processes this request via RequestDispatcher.forward(), instead of instantiating and calling the Action class specified by the type attribute. The forwards define the return values from the Action.

There can be only one forward, include, or type specified in the forward method call. Keep in mind that there can be many forwards per action. The include attribute is the same except it processes the request using RequestDispatcher.include().

The multipartClass is the fully qualified Java class name of the MultipartRequestHandler implementation class used to process multipart request data for this Action. MultipartRequest-Handler provides a standard interface for Struts to deal with file uploads from forms with enctypes of "multipart/form-data."

The parameter attribute is a general-purpose configuration parameter that can be used to pass extra information to the Action instance selected by this Action. It's possible to access the parameter's value within the Action class via the mapping.getParameter() method. An example of a use for the parameter attribute is to indicate what step in a wizard you are processing. While there can be only one parameter attribute per action, it is possible to specify more than a single parameter value by using a delimiter to separate the values like

```
<action ...  parameter="param1;param2;param3" />
```

or specify key-value pairs like

```
<action ...  parameter="key1=value1;key2=value2;key3=value3" />.
```

Basically, you can use the parameter attribute however you like as long as you write whatever code is necessary to parse the string if there is more than one value. This is useful if you have several related tasks using a parameter to distinguish them. There is a good sample of a helper class to tokenize parameters from the action mapping in the Struts contrib folder in the Scaffold source code example. The class is org.apache.scaffold.http.HelperAction in the perform() method if you want to reference it.

The prefix and suffix attributes are used to match request parameter names to form Bean property names. A comma-delimited list of security role names allowed to request this Action can be specified using the roles attribute. If you need to access the set of security role names used to authorize access to this Action, call the getRolesNames() method on the ActionConfig object and an array will be returned.

If the unknown attribute is set to "true" for an action mapping, that indicates that it should be the default action for the application. It is considered good practice to use action mappings for everything that needs to be done through the application. This guarantees that the request will pass through the controller and that it sticks to the MVC model. Therefore, you should have at least one unknown attribute set for an action mapping so that there is a default action mapping.

It's possible to tailor actions for specific tasks. For example, say that you have two different actions that both use the same ActionForm, but only one of the actions requires the validation to be performed. This can easily be configured in the sample action mapping as

```
<action
 path="/search"
```

```
 type="cdmanager.actions.Search"
 name="cdForm"
 scope="request"
 validate="false">
</action>

<action
 path="/insert"
 type="cdmanager.actions.Insert"
 name="cdForm"
 scope="request"
 validate="true"
 input="/Insert.jsp"">
 <forward name="success" path="/confirm.jsp"/>
</action>
```

In this sample, we have two different actions that both use the cdForm to gather data. On the search action, we don't want to validate the form, but on the insert we do so that the user doesn't try to insert bad data.

### 6.2.6 Controller Configuration

A primary design goal in the Struts 1.1 release is that the struts-config.xml for an existing 1.0.x Struts application can be used as a subapplication with no changes. Due to support for the subapps, all the context-relative values in struts-config.xml are now actually application relative. The implication this has is that a request URI is now a concatenation of the context path plus the application prefix plus the local value. This works even for the default subapplication because its prefix is a zero-length string. This is the reason the application-specific attributes have been moved into this struts-config.xml file from the web.xml where they used to live in Struts 1.0.x. However, the existing init params are still recognized for the default subapplication.

There is a <controller> element to specify the controller configuration for requests directed to this application. There are a number of attributes that can be specified in this element. These are listed in the Table 6.2.

If you create a custom RequestProcessor, you specify it in each struts-config.xml where it is needed, as in

```
<controller processorClass="classname" />
```

where classname is the fully qualified class name. The default processorClass is org.apache.struts.action.RequestProcessor.

The RequestProcessor contains the processing logic that the Struts controller servlet performs as it receives each servlet request from the container. It is possible to override any of the methods that you need to customize. Usually this will be the processPreprocess() method, which is a general-purpose preprocessing hook. The RequestProcessor

**Table 6.2:** Attributes of `<controller>` element.

| Attribute | Purpose | Default value |
|---|---|---|
| `bufferSize` | The size of the input buffer used when processing file uploads | 4096 |
| `className` | Implementation subclass of the standard configuration Bean, if you do not want to use the standard value | `org.apache.struts.config.ControllerConfig` |
| `contentType` | Default content type (and optional character encoding) to be set on each response; may be overridden by a forward to Servlet or JSP | text/html |
| `debug` | Debugging detail level for this application | 0 |
| `locale` | Set to true if you want a Locale object stored in the user's session if not already present | True |
| `maxFileSize` | The maximum size (in bytes) of a file to be accepted as a file upload; can be expressed as a number followed by a K, M, or G, which are interpreted to mean kilobytes, megabytes, or gigabytes, respectively | 250M |
| `multipartClass` | The fully qualified Java class name of the multipart request handler class to be used | `org.apache.struts.upload .DiskMultipartRequestHandler` |
| `nocache` | Set to true if you want Struts to add HTTP headers for defeating caching to every response | False |
| `processorClass` | The fully qualified Java class name of the `RequestProcessor` class to be used | `org.apache.struts.action.RequestProcessor` |
| `tempDir` | Temporary working directory to use when processing file uploads | Directory provided by servlet container |

is an implementation of the intercepting filter design pattern that allows for preprocessing and postprocessing of a request. Using this design pattern enables filters to process common services that might be required in an application without having to make changes to core request processing code. Some examples of what might be considered common services include

- Client authentication
- Valid client session
- Constraints that might be applicable to request paths
- Browser version or type support
- Logging information

A situation where you might want to create your own custom RequestProcessor class is if you wanted to check for a valid session attribute to ensure that a user is logged into the application. We've already talked about doing a check in either the Action or a custom tag. This is another alternative. You can check the session for something that your logon action should have already put there. If it's there, return super.processPreprocess(). If it's not, return mapping.findForward("logon"), assuming you have a global forward in your struts-config.xml called "logon."

While it's also possible to do this type of checking in a base class for your Actions, the advantage of doing it in the processPreprocess() method is that it is called before the ActionForm validate() and the Action execute() methods.

The declaration of the <controller> element must be done after action-mapping declarations. It should be the last element in the struts-config.xml file unless you also have PlugIns defined. A sample <controller> element is

```
<controller
   processorClass="cdmanager.framework.CustomRequestProcessor"
   debug="2"
   nocache="true" />
```

### 6.2.7 Defining a PlugIn

A new feature of Struts 1.1 is the ablity to define a PlugIn. A PlugIn is a configuration wrapper for an application-specific module or service that must be notified about application startup and application shutdown events. These events correspond to the container calls init() and destroy() on the corresponding ActionServlet instance that allows a module to be called without the need to subclass ActionServlet for simply Servlet lifecycle activities.

PlugIn modules can be configured in the struts-config.xml file using the <plug-in> element. Classes that implement the PlugIn interface must supply a zero-argument constructor for use by ActionServlet. Configuration can be accomplished by providing standard JavaBeans property setter methods that will all have been called before the init() method was invoked. An instance of the specified class is created for each element, and can be configured with nested <set-property> elements. For example, in the struts-config.xml, we might have the last entry defined as

```
<plug-in className="org.apache.struts.validator.action.ValidatorPlugIn">
    <set-property property="pathname" value="/WEB-INF/validator-rules.xml"/>
    <set-property property="pathname" value="/WEB-INF/validation.xml"/>
  </plug-in>
```

This means that two instances of the `ValidatorPlugIn` will be created, each setting the property pathname to the appropriate value. We will take a closer look at the `ValidatorPlugIn` in Chapter 11, but it was important at this juncture to show a sample of how a PlugIn might be used.

## 6.3 Summary

Chapter 6 showed how to set up and configure both your web application using the `web.xml` file and the Struts-specific pieces using the `struts-config.xml` file. It further demonstrated how to create subapplications as well as how to set up and configure the Controller component. Last, it provided details about the available elements and attributes to define data sources, form Beans, global forwards, and action mappings. Between these two files, an entire web application flow can be defined and used for processing.

chapter 7

# Building Struts-Enabled JSPs

Throughout this book, we have been talking about various Struts components and how to create and use them. Interwoven throughout the discussion has been the use of JavaServer Pages. This chapter covers how to build Struts-enabled JSPs and is kept intentionally short. Primarily, I want to make sure that it's understood where the taglib issues fit into the Struts world. The next chapter will go into details about how to actually use and apply the custom tags provided with Struts.

The only thing that really makes a JSP Struts enabled is the use of the various custom tags that are available. Custom tags are usually distributed in the form of a tag library. The tag library defines a set of related custom tags and contains the objects that implement the tags. These objects are called the tag handlers. If you wanted to build straight HTML files without using the Struts custom tag libraries, you can do so. However, I'll show why you would want to use them, and how to do it. While it is entirely possible that you might need to build some of your own custom tags and include them in your defined tag library, we are not going to go into detail about this since it is beyond the scope of this book. However, an application-specific sample of a custom tag library is included with our sample application in case you are interested. If you need more details about how to build your custom tags, refer to the tutorial located at *java.sun.com/products/jsp/tutorial/TagLibrariesTOC.html.*

The main purpose of the JSP technology is to provide dynamic content and to separate content generation and business logic from presentation. It does so by taking advantage of reusable tags and Objects, both of which simplify the maintenance of web applications. We will be going into the details of the Struts custom tag libraries in this chapter. I am assuming that you have a good working knowledge of JSP technology. If you need to brush up on the basics or are interested in reading the full specification, it can be found at *java.sun.com/products/jsp/download.html.* If you want a quick and handy reference card on JSP syntax, you can download it from *java.sun.com/products/jsp/technical.html#syntax.*

With that said, let's get started using JSPs and the Struts custom tag libraries in your projects.

## 7.1 Setting Up a JSP

It is possible to have a JSP that doesn't include any of the Struts custom tag libraries but that is still used within framework. There can be a JSP that is identified in an action mapping, a confirmation page, or an error page that is used on its own.

There are a number of reasons for using the available tag libraries. The first is that they provide a consistent way to build your pages. By using not only the available Struts custom tag libraries, but other tag libraries such as those available from the Jakarta Taglibs project *(jakarta.apache.org/taglibs/index.html)* or in the JSP Standard Tag Library (JSTL) *(java.sun.com/products/jsp/taglibraries.html#jstl)*, the JSP becomes more readable and therefore more maintainable.

While this might not seem like a big deal, when you're working on a large-scale web application where you can have more than a few dozen JSP files, this issue deserves consideration.

Next, by using the custom tags, you will save yourself—and your development team—time from reinventing the wheel for functionality that might already exist. And it might have already been tested, too.

Third, functionality provided in the custom tags already takes into consideration some of the features of the Struts framework. This includes internationalization, as well as ease of use of working with Beans in your pages. So, to conclude this discussion, it is usually worthwhile and time saving to use custom tags. The question then becomes, how do you use them?

### 7.1.1 Making Tags Available

Making custom tags available to your pages is simple. First, the custom tag library must be made available for your application. This is done by using the `<taglib>` element in your `web.xml` file.

```
<taglib>
    <taglib-uri>/WEB-INF/struts-bean.tld</taglib-uri>
    <taglib-location>/WEB-INF/struts-bean.tld</taglib-location>
  </taglib>
```

There is a `<taglib>` element for every tag library that you plan to make available in your application. It doesn't matter whether it's a tag library that you created yourself or if it's one provided from a third party (like Struts or Jakarta). It is usually easiest to just include a `<taglib>` entry for all the available taglibs, even if you don't initially think that you will be using them. There really is no substantial overhead associated with having them declared in the `web.xml`.

Next, you need to make the tags themselves available on the JSP that will use them. This is done using the JSP `taglib` directive. This directive defines a tag library and the prefix that is used for the custom tags in the JSP. The `taglib` directive must be specified before any of the custom tags are used in a JSP. It's possible to use more than one `taglib` directive in a JSP, but the prefix defined in each must be unique. A sample use of this directive follows:

```
<%@ taglib uri="/WEB-INF/struts-bean.tld" prefix="bean" %>
```

The URI attribute is the Uniform Resource Identifier (URI) that uniquely locates the TLD that describes the set of custom tags associated with the named tag prefix. If the URI is a pathname, it is interpreted relative to the root of the web application and should resolve to a TLD file directly or to a JAR file that has a TLD file at location META-INF/taglib.tld. The prefix is what is used to reference a custom tag from that library.

For example, <bean:message /> refers to the custom tag message as defined in the Bean library that was declared in the preceding sample. You can name your prefix anything you like; however, it makes more sense to call it something logical so that your custom tags can be read easily. Prefixes can't be empty, and you can't use any of the following: jsp, jspx, java, javax, servlet, sun, and sunw. These prefixes are reserved by Sun Microsystems. Anything else is fair game, but use common sense.

## 7.2 Taglib Definitions

In any given application, even with the best-laid design plans and intentions, what starts out small has a way of ending up bigger than you expected. This is usually the result of a variety of factors. User requirements become better defined as development progresses, changes occur in design strategies, new functionality becomes required, and so on. Because of this fact of development life, I always like to plan ahead and always act as though things are going to grow and need to be easily maintained. Therefore, it's better to keep things organized. A big step in that organizational direction comes in the form of taglib definitions.

As we've seen, it's possible to use a custom tag library from a variety of sources: those that you build yourself or those you get from third parties. It is possible to—and many people do—just add the taglib directive to each and every JSP that will use a particular tag library. I find it easier to manage if you have one JSP file that contains all the taglibs that you will be using in your application. Doing it this way results in several benefits. One is that all JSPs will use prefixes consistently throughout the application. Another is that if revisions of taglibs change and you need to point to different TLD files, the change can be done in one place instead of throughout various JSPs. The way to accomplish this is to have one JSP (I call it taglib.jsp in our sample application code) that looks something like this:

```
<!-- Listing of all of the taglibs that we reference in this application -->
<!-- Struts provided Taglibs -->
<%@ taglib uri="/WEB-INF/struts-bean.tld" prefix="bean" %>
<%@ taglib uri="/WEB-INF/struts-html.tld" prefix="html" %>
<!-- Application-specific Taglibs -->
<%@ taglib uri="/WEB-INF/app.tld" prefix="app" %>
```

That way, all that must be added is

```
<%@ include file="/WEB-INF/taglibs.jsp" %>
```

at the top of each JSP in the application. There. Your application maintenance has just been simplified. While there is no real performance penalty that I've noticed for the additional include, even if there was, the maintenance issue takes priority.

Once all of your taglib directives have been set up, you are ready to use the custom tags. Chapter 8 explores the various custom tags provided by Struts along with how to use them.

## 7.3 Summary

JSPs are the main View objects of the MVC architecture used in Struts. A number of custom tag libraries are available that can be used in your development to make life easier, and they can come from a variety of sources. It is simple to add in tag library references if you maintain your applications using a single file to define those libraries.

chapter 8

# Working with the Struts Custom Tag Libraries

Now that you understand how to get the custom tag libraries into your JSP files, it's time to put the pedal to the metal. If you equate this book to a good meal, get ready for the main course. There are quite a few tags provided in a number of Struts libraries. We will walk through the tag libraries, explore what is available, and then look at how to use the most popular tags by examining tags from our sample application. This chapter is the longest in the book, but don't be intimidated. There's a lot to know about these tag libraries, and the more comfortable you are working with the various tag libraries, the more powerful your JSPs will be and the quicker you will be able to develop them.

There are five tag libraries available with Struts 1.1. Each library contains multiple tags. The name and general purpose of each are

- *Struts-html.* Tags useful for creating dynamic HTML user interfaces and including input forms.
- *Struts-bean.* Tags useful for defining new Beans, in any scope, from a variety of possible sources.
- *Struts-logic.* Tags useful for manipulating presentation logic without the use of scriptlets.
- *Struts-nested.* Tags useful for extending the current Struts tags to allow for nesting. This library provides the ability to define a nested object model, represent, and also manage that model.
- *Struts-template.* Tags useful for creating dynamic JSP templates for pages that share a common format.

Some of the tags that are available in Struts have a very good chance of becoming part of the Jakarta Taglibs project, or even deprecated because the functionality might appear in the JSP Standard Tag Library (JSTL). Just be aware that this is a fluid chapter, but it should give you a good understanding about how to use the tags regardless of where they exist at the time you read this. Also, there are a variety of tag libraries offered on the Resources page on the Struts site that are provided by engineers like you and me who have written useful tags. I won't be going into details about those, but I encourage you to check out what's available. There is some useful stuff up there.

In short, it's possible that by the time this book goes to press there could be more tag libraries, but I'll work with what is available now. So, let's begin examining some common aspects of the libraries and then we'll look at each library in turn.

## 8.1 When Tags Throw Exceptions

It's always possible at some point when using tags to make a mistake. If a tag is used incorrectly by way of specifying the wrong attributes, a `JspException` will be thrown at runtime. As with any JSP that has the potential to throw exceptions, it is recommended that an error page be declared so that if an exception is thrown, at least it will be directed to an error page. This is done by using the JSP `<%@ page %>` directive. It's possible to then process the exception thrown by the tag on the error page by accessing the attribute key `org.apache.struts.action.EXCEPTION_KEY` in the request. For example, I've added the page directive into the `taglib.jsp` so that it is available for all JSPs as follows:

```
<!-- Common error page for all JSPs -->
<%@ page errorPage="/errorpage.jsp" %>
```

Then I have created an `errorpage.jsp` that includes the following code snippet:

```
javax.servlet.jsp.JspException jspException =
(javax.servlet.jsp.JspException)(request.getAttribute(Action.EXCEPTION_KEY));
if (jspException != null){
            message = ((Exception)jspException).getMessage();
}
```

For the full code that formats and prints out the exception stack, reference the file in the sample download. By using this mechanism, you will at least get a reasonable error message displayed if your tag throws an exception.

## 8.2 Using Property Referencing

Tags (in both the Struts-html and Struts-bean libraries) that support the `property` attribute generally support simple, nested, and indexed references. A simple reference is similar to the syntax of the standard `<jsp:getProperty>`, `<jsp:setProperty>`. Using the standard JavaBeans naming conventions (see *java.sun.com/products/javabeans* for the complete specification), the `getFoo()` and `setFoo(fooValue)` method calls are made. Additional support included with Struts is its use of the standard Java reflection (in the `PropertyUtils` class) and Introspection APIs to identify the names of the actual property getter and setter methods. This allows customized method names to be specified in a BeanInfo class.

Nested references allow for dot notation. It is possible to access a property through a hierarchy of property names separated by periods (.). For example, the getter of the following property reference property="foo.bar" is translated into the equivalent Java code getFoo().getBar().

When processing an input form where the setter method is called on a nested reference, the entry in the chain is the one that has the value passed to it. So the Java code would resemble

```
getFoo().setBar(value)
```

Indexed references are used if a properties value is an array; then subscripts can be used to access the individual elements. This type of reference is also used when the JavaBean offers indexed getter/setter methods. So property="foo[3]" translates to getFoo(3). The corresponding setter would translate to setFoo(3,value). When using an indexed reference, always follow zero-based indexing.

It is possible to use a combination of reference types where both nested and indexed properties are used arbitrarily. An example of this is foo.bar[0].

Be careful because if you get the syntax wrong or you don't have the Bean methods set up correctly, JSP runtime exceptions will be thrown.

## 8.3 Using the Struts-html Tag Library

The tags implemented in the Struts-html taglib are used to create Struts input forms as well as HTML-based user interfaces. As a reference, the available tags in the html library are shown in Table 8.1. We will look at some of the common tags specifically with examples.

One might ask, why would you want to use a set of custom tag libraries for basically duplicating many HTML elements? That was the first thing that popped into my mind when I started working with the Struts tags. It turns out, there are a number of reasons for it. One of the main reasons involves the internationalization tags for non-form-related tags. If your site is implemented in several languages, all of your images and text come from ResourceBundles. Struts is already aware of these bundles and will display the right content for the specified locale. The <html:img> and the <html:errors> tags are good examples of this.

A second reason for using such tags is their ease of use. The tags provide a clean approach to coding in the JSPs, and they keep the pages readable. Upon further examination, some of the tags provide additional functionality that the developer doesn't have to worry about. An example of this is when using the <html:link> tag. This tag automatically handles URL rewriting of the jsessionid for users who do not support cookies. So as you can see, there is more to the html tags than meets the eye, or to be precise, than meets the page.

While it's possible that some of the extra functionality provided in the tags might not be useful to your project, chances are that many of the tags will be. It's also possible to use some of the tags and not others. So the choice is really up to each developer to use the tags as he or she sees fit.

**Table 8.1:** Struts-html tag reference.

| Tag name | Rendering description |
|---|---|
| base | HTML <base> element |
| button | Button input field |
| cancel | Cancel button |
| checkbox | Checkbox input field |
| errors | Conditionally display a set of accumulated error messages |
| file | File select input field |
| form | Define an input form |
| hidden | Hidden field |
| html | HTML <html> element |
| image | Input tag of type image |
| img | HTML img tag |
| link | HTML anchor or hyperlink |
| messages | Conditionally display a set of accumulated messages |
| multibox | Checkbox input field |
| option | Select option |
| options | Collection of select options |
| optionsCollection | Collection of select options |
| password | Password input field |
| radio | Radio button input field |
| reset | Reset button input field |
| rewrite | Render a URI |
| select | Select element |
| submit | Submit button |
| text | Input field of type text |
| textarea | Input field of type textarea |

Space dictates that it's not possible to provide samples for each and every tag that is available, so let's pick a few of the more common and useful tags from the HTML library and walk through them.

### 8.3.1 Using and Accessing Form-Related Tags

Many of the HTML tags work within the context of an `<html:form>` tag. The form tag outputs a standard HTML form tag, but more important, links the input form with an `ActionForm` object. The appropriate Bean class to associate the subclassed `ActionForm` is specified either as a property to the form tag or in the `struts-config.xml` in the action mapping. Each field on the input form should correspond to a property in the ActionForm Bean instance. Using reflection, when a form field and Bean property correspond, the Bean is first used to populate the form if the Bean is already in scope, and then to store the user's input when the form is submitted to the controller servlet.

The form tag specifies the action that the controller dispatches to by using the action attribute. For example, in our login.jsp we have

```
<html:form action="/logon" focus="userName">... </html:form>
```

When a submit is done on this form, the logon action mapping (as defined in the struts-config.xml) is used by the controller to determine the default attribute values for name, scope, type, etc. The focus is used to set the current focus to the specified field.

Each of the tags that relate to form fields has a set of common attributes that can be set on any of the tags. These attributes include

- *name.* The ActionForm Bean associated with this form.
- *property.* Name of the request parameter that is included with this submission, set to the specified value.
- *value.* The value of the label to be used with this element and the value of the specified request parameter.
- All of the ten or more JavaScript event handlers (onclick, onfocus, onchange, etc.).
- *accesskey.* The keyboard character used to move focus immediately to this element.
- *tabindex.* The tab order on the form for this element.
- *style.* CSS styles to be applied to this HTML element.
- *styleClass.* CSS style sheet class to be applied to this HTML element.

Looking at Table 8.1, it's clear that any of the other form input fields you'd expect are available.

As an example, if you want to have multiple checkboxes on a form, you can define your ActionForm to have methods like

```
public void setMyParams( String[] myParams ) {...}
public String[] getMyParams() {...}
```

and the Form Bean should be populated with the correct parameter values. This is helpful for HTTP parameters that can have more than one value. Then you can define checkboxes in your form like

```
<html:multibox property="myParam" value="one" />
<html:multibox property="myParam" value="two" />
<html:multibox property="myParam" value="three" />
```

A call to getMyParams() from your Action would return an array containing the Strings "one" and "two" if you had both of those checked on your html form.

## 8.3.2 Working with Errors and Messages

The <html:errors> tag is used to conditionally display a set of error messages. These messages are errors that have been set by our Action classes by using

```
ActionErrors errors = new ActionErrors();
```

followed by something similar to

```
errors.add(ActionErrors.GLOBAL_ERROR, new ActionError("error.database.missing"));
```

The saveErrors() method on the Action class is called to save the specified error messages keys.

```
if (!errors.empty()) {
       saveErrors(request, errors);
}
```

The message keys are contained in the ActionErrors object and placed in the appropriate request attribute. The request attribute key is Action.ERROR_KEY that resolves to "org.apache.struts.action.ERROR." This attribute key is what allows the tag to gain access to the errors that are set.

If the ActionErrors Bean is not found by the JSP, nothing will be rendered on the JSP when using the <html:errors> tag. In order to use this tag successfully, you must have defined an application scope MessageResources Bean under the default attribute name that contains at least errors.header and errors.footer message keys. These keys from our ApplicationResources file look like

```
errors.header=<h3><font color="red">Validation
Error</font></h3>You must correct the following error(s) before proceeding:<ul>
errors.footer=</ul><hr>
```

It is typical to use <ul></ul> in the header/footer to engender the display of a bulleted list of errors, but it's totally up to you how to format the header and footer. Some HTML tags are included just as examples for how to highlight error messages, but it is up to you how you want to display the errors.

The <html:messages> tag makes it easy to send both informational messages and errors to the same page at the same time. You can then render them differently if you want. Messages (ActionMessages object) are an encapsulation of an individual message (ActionMessage object). The message consists of a message key that is used to look up message text in an appropriate message resources database or file. Each message has up to four placeholder objects that can be used for parametric replacement in the message text.

Working similarly to errors, messages can also be set in an ActionForm class, Action class, or business logic component and stored as an ActionMessages object, ActionErrors object, a string, or a string array in the request scope. If such an ActionMessages Bean is not found, nothing will be rendered. To use this tag, you must define an application scope MessageResources Bean under the default attribute name.

Messages can be used for various confirmations such as after a record has been added or updated, as in the following snippet from our sample application:

```
ActionMessages actionMessages = new ActionMessages();
actionMessages.add(ActionMessages.GLOBAL_MESSAGE,
                   new ActionMESSAGE("record.inserted"));
return (mapping.findForward(Globals.FORWARD_CONFIRMATION));
```

The JSP that is being forwarded to just includes the following tag to render the message:

```
<html:messages/>
```

If you use messages for confirmations, make sure that there isn't also other information on the page that might require the user to refresh. If there is, then you are better off redirecting to a status message page instead of forwarding because if a refresh is done on the original page, it might cause a repost, which is probably not what you want. But remember, on a redirect you get a new request so the ActionMessage in the request scope will be gone. One possible way to get around this is to create an Object in session scope, and then access this object from your status message page. Then when you're done, remove the object from the session.

### 8.3.3 Completed Sample

Let's look at a complete sample using our `logon.jsp` from the sample application. This particular JSP uses a variety of tags from the html library so you can see them in action. I'll skip over explaining any of the standard html code so as not to bore you.

First, we have the JSP directive to set the scriptlet language, and then we include our common `taglib.jsp` file. This is the file that contains the listing of all the taglibs we'll be using.

```
<%@ page language="java" %>
<%@ include file="taglibs.jsp" %>
```

Then we set the html element with language attributes extracted from the user's current `Locale` object, if there is one. The locale is set to "true" to indicate that if there is no locale set, a Locale should be recorded based on the current request's `Accept-Language` header.

```
<html:html locale="true">
<head>
<html:base/>
```

If you use relative links in your page, you should place the `<html:base/>` tag inside the `<head>` element of your page. It will render a base tag so that relative links will not appear to be broken. The Bean tag library is used (we'll be talking about it more in a minute) to get a message from the `ApplicationResource` file based on the message key provided. This is the crux of using internationalized messages strings. The `<html:base>` tag renders an HTML `<base>` element with an `href` attribute pointing to the absolute location of the JSP. We use this tag because it allows us to use relative URL references in the page that are calculated based on the URL of the page itself. Usually, the browser would normally resolve relative paths against the URL to which the most recent submit took place. In particular, this makes things like relative URIs in an <img> element resolve against the URI of the JSP even though the URI of the controller is still showing in the location bar.

```
<title><bean:message key="logon.title"/></title>
</head>
<body bgcolor="white">
```

The next line is interesting because it shows how you can mix and match standard HTML code with Struts tags. We are displaying an image, but we're allowing the message to be pulled from the resource file, so the alt description is displayed in the appropriate language.

```
<img src="sblogo.gif" alt="<bean:message key="image.switchback"/>" align="left"/>
```

Display any error messages that were set by our Action class.

```
<html:errors/>

<html:form action="/logon" focus="userName">
<table border="0" width="100%">
  <tr>
    <th align="right">
      <bean:message key="prompt.username"/>
    </th>
    <td align="left">
```

Our first input field is a text field. The name we use for the property value is the same name that must be used in the ActionForm Bean for the setter/getter methods in JavaBean naming convention format, that is, setUserName(value), getUserName().

```
      <html:text property="userName" size="15" maxlength="15"/>
    </td>
  </tr>

  <tr>
    <th align="right">
      <bean:message key="prompt.password"/>
    </th>
    <td align="left">
```

The next input field is a password field. The redisplay attribute indicates whether or not existing values will be redisplayed if they exist. Since this is a password field, redisplayed values show as asterisks on the visible page. However, the clear text of the actual password value will be visible though the Show Page Source menu option of the client browser if redisplay is set to true. Since this is a Logon page, we don't want the password visible at all, so we set redisplay to false. Setting the redisplay to false actually causes the password field to be left empty.

```
      <html:password property="password" size="15" maxlength="15"
                     redisplay="false"/>
```

```
    </td>
  </tr>

  <tr>
    <td align="right">
```

Then we have our normal submit and reset buttons. The `property` attribute on the submit form is important so that your Action class can use it to figure out what logic must be executed. The `value` property is used both to label the button and to set the value of the field. In this sample, we are setting this value by using an internationalized string from the resource file. We could simply have a `value="Logon"` property, but creating the button the way it's shown will create fewer headaches when your boss tells you your application has to ship to China . . . right now. The Logon page will be rendered as shown in Figure 8.1.

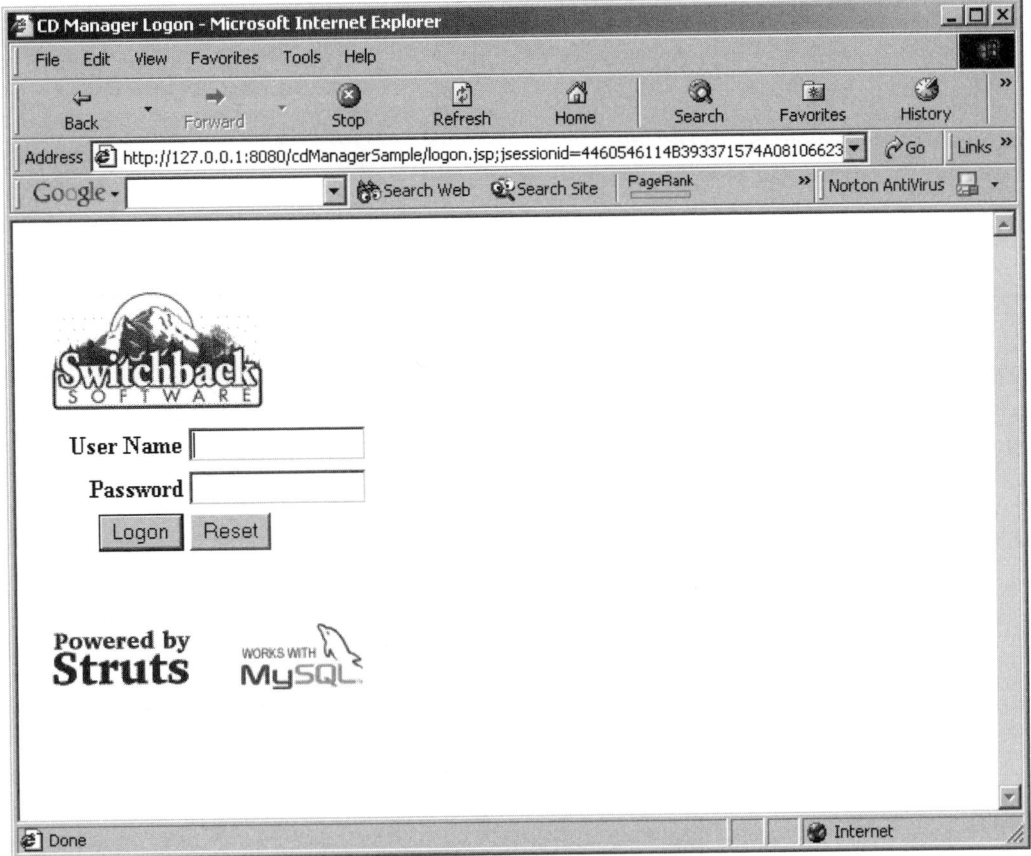


**Figure 8.1:** Logon screenshot.

The property attribute can be helpful in determining logic because if you have multiple submit buttons on a form, you can set the property value to be the same for all of them. Then when the form is submitted, check the value field to see which action was performed and what needs to be executed.

Another advantage worth pointing out about using the <bean:message> for the value is that if you have multiple submit buttons, and you are doing comparisons, you can simply do a lookup on the message key in your Action class and you'll be guaranteed that your comparisons are correct, regardless of the language the application is running in.

```
<html:submit property="action" >
      <bean:message key="button.logon"/>
</html:submit>
    </td>
    <td align="left">
      <html:reset/>
    </td>
  </tr>

</table>
```

Lastly, we close out our form, and page.

```
</html:form>
</body>
</html:html>
```

## 8.4 Using the Struts-bean Tag Library

The Struts-bean tag library contains tags that are used to manipulate Beans. This includes Bean creation, in all scopes, as well as rendering tags for specific Bean properties. JavaBeans play an important role in JSP technology as probably the main component model. Many of you might already be familiar with the standard <jsp:useBean> tag. This tag is used to create a Bean and create named scripting variables that are accessed within a scriptlet.

The same question that we applied to the Struts-html library might apply here. Why do I need another set of tags to duplicate functionality already provided in a standard JSP tag? The answer (again) is that the Struts-bean tags provide a number of enhancements to the basics provided by <jsp:useBean>. However, if you are going to want to use <jsp:getProperty> or <jsp:setProperty>, you have to have the reference created using <jsp:useBean>.

The first reason for using the Struts-bean tags over <jsp:useBean> is the extended syntax available for Bean properties. The extended syntax (which we discussed in Section 8.2) allows properties to be references using simple, nested, and indexed names. Second, it's possible to automatically create new Beans in any scope from a variety of objects (such as headers, parameters, cookies) and APIs associated with the current request or servlet container with a

**Table 8.2:** Struts-bean tag reference.

| Tag name | Description |
|---|---|
| cookie | Define a scripting variable based on the value(s) of the specified request cookie |
| define | Define a scripting variable based on the value(s) of the specified Bean property |
| header | Define a scripting variable based on the value(s) of the specified request header |
| include | Load the response from a dynamic application request and make it available as a Bean |
| message | Render an internationalized message string to the response |
| page | Expose a specified item from the page context as a Bean |
| parameter | Define a scripting variable based on the value(s) of the specified request parameter |
| resource | Load a web application resource and make it available as a Bean |
| size | Define a Bean containing the number of elements in a collection or map |
| struts | Expose a named Struts internal configuration object as a Bean |
| write | Render the value of the specified Bean property to the current JspWriter |

simple tag. Third, it's possible to render textual output from a Bean that can be included in the JSP response. Table 8.2 shows the tags available.

All the Struts-bean tags share a common set of tag attributes.

- *id.* Names the scripting variable as well as the key value used to locate this Bean in the scope defined by the scope attribute.
- *name.* Defines the key value by which an existing Bean will be looked up in the scope defined by the scope attribute.
- *property.* Defines the name of a JavaBeans property, of the JSP Bean identified by the name, and (optionally) the scope attributes.
- *scope.* Identifies the JSP scope ("page," "request," "session," or "application") within which a particular Bean is searched for using the key specified (by the `name` attribute), or created (under the key specified by the `id` attribute). The default is page scope.

Let's look at how we use some of the Struts-bean tags.

## 8.4.1 Using Bean Tags

`<bean:define>` is a tag that serves a few purposes: creation of new Beans, copying other Beans, or copying just a property of another Bean. Beans created default to page scope unless you specify otherwise by using the `scope` attribute. A good example of using `<bean:define>` is this. Let's say you have accomplished some business logic in a Bean in your Action class. Then you want to save this information, in whatever scope is appropriate, for later access through a JSP. The code in the Action class might look something akin to

```
MyBean myBean = new MyBean();
myBean.setResult("some result");
session.setAttribute("result", myBean);
```

Then it's possible to write JSP scriplet code for pulling out the attribute and then making the appropriate method call on the Bean.

```
<%
MyBean myBean = (MyBean)session.getAttribute("result");
if(myBean!=null) {
String result = myBean.getResult();
%>
```

Then you do something appropriate with the result in your JSP. The problem with this is that you included scriplet code into your JSP files, which is something that is best avoided for the reasons discussed earlier in the book.

A better way to do this is to use the <bean:define> tag by including something like

```
<logic:present name='result'>
    <bean:define  id='myBean' name='result'  scope='session'
                  toScope='page' type='MyBean' />
        <bean:include id='myResult' page='<%= myBean.getResult() %>' />
</logic:present>
```

This makes the Bean and all of its methods available to the JSP and accessible throughout your JSP.

The id is the name of the scripting variable being created, and the name is used to locate the object in the scope specified. The toScope is used to determine what scope the new Bean should be created in, and the type is the class name of the type of Bean to create. In this sample, we also used the <bean:include> to make a dynamic call to the Bean and then we stored the return in a scripting variable myResult. myResult is then used as <% myResult %> when needed. Notice we are using a tag from the Struts-logic tag library, <logic:present>, because if the Bean has not been placed in one of the scopes of the JSP, we don't want to execute this code.

Similar functionally holds for the other Bean tags that have to do with creating scripting variables: cookies, header, page, and parameter. It is possible to create Beans from any of these objects by using the appropriate tag. For example, if you are passing a query parameter to a JSP, you can use

```
<logic:present parameter="query">
<bean:parameter id="query" name="query"/>
    Query parameter = <%=query%>
</logic:present>
```

We can also combine Bean tags, for example, <bean:cookie> and <bean:write>. We use <bean:cookie> to get a cookie value in a request and then access the values using the <bean:write> tag. The <bean:write> retrieves the value of the specified Bean property, and then renders it to the current JspWriter as a String. We create a scripting variable called myCookie that is looked up using the standard JSESSIONID. We default the value to UNDEFINED if it doesn't exist. Then we access a few of the properties that are associated with cookies to print their values.

This tag understands the syntax for the simple, nested, and indexed property references that we've discussed. Notice that we have set ignore to "true." The reason is that if the property doesn't exist, then the <bean:write> will throw an exception. To prevent this exception, we must change ignore's default value, which is "false," to "true."

```
<bean:cookie id="myCookie" name="JSESSIONID" value="UNDEFINED"/>
<bean:write name="myCookie" property="name" ignore="true"/>
<bean:write name="myCookie" property="maxAge" ignore="true"/>
```

The <bean:message> tag also writes to the JspWriter. This tag is used to render an internationalized message. You'll recall (I hope) that we have seen this tag a few times in samples already. The <bean:message> tag retrieves a message for the locale specified using a message key. There can be up to five parametric replacements. This is why you see {0} or {1} in the message resource files. These are placeholders for parameters that might be passed in. Messages can be retrieved by using the attribute key, or retrieved directly from the resource file, or retrieved indirectly using the name and property attributes to get the value from a Bean. We demonstrate both uses.

```
<bean:message key="button.Login">;

<bean:message key="message.welcome" arg0='<%= user.getUserName() %>'>;
```

## 8.5 Using the Struts-logic Tag Library

The tags in the Struts-logic tag library are used to make a best effort to keep scriplets out of your JSPs. These tags are used to perform conditionals, looping, and basically anything that requires iteration. These tags provide four basic groups of functionality.

- Value comparisons
- Substring matching
- Presentation location
- Collection manipulation

Table 8.3 shows all the available tags in the logic library.

Let's look at some of the tags in each of these categories. The sample code included here is available for viewing and running from the Logic Samples link on the Main Menu of our sample application.

**Table 8.3:** Struts-logic tag reference.

| Tag name | Description |
|---|---|
| `empty` | Evaluate the nested body content of this tag if the requested variable is either null or an empty string |
| `equal` | Evaluate the nested body content of this tag if the requested variable is equal to the specified value |
| `forward` | Forward control to the page specified by the specified ActionForward entry |
| `greaterEqual` | Evaluate the nested body content of this tag if the requested variable is greater than or equal to the specified value |
| `greaterThan` | Evaluate the nested body content of this tag if the requested variable is greater than the specified value |
| `iterate` | Repeat the nested body content of this tag over a specified collection |
| `lessEqual` | Evaluate the nested body content of this tag if the requested variable is greater than or equal to the specified value |
| `lessThan` | Evaluate the nested body content of this tag if the requested variable is less than the specified value |
| `match` | Evaluate the nested body content of this tag if the specified value is an appropriate substring of the requested variable |
| `messagesNotPresent` | Generate the nested body content of this tag if the specified message is not present in this request |
| `messagesPresent` | Generate the nested body content of this tag if the specified message is present in this request |
| `notEmpty` | Evaluate the nested body content of this tag if the requested variable is neither null nor an empty string |
| `notEqual` | Evaluate the nested body content of this tag if the requested variable is not equal to the specified value |
| `notMatch` | Evaluate the nested body content of this tag if the specified value is not an appropriate substring of the requested variable |
| `notPresent` | Generate the nested body content of this tag if the specified value is not present in this request |
| `present` | Generate the nested body content of this tag if the specified value is present in this request |
| `redirect` | Render an HTTP redirect |

## 8.5.1 Value Comparisons

It is often necessary to do some type of value comparison of property values. The comparison tags are comprised of `equal`, `notEqual`, `greaterEqual`, `lessEqual`, `greaterThan`, `lessThan`, `present`, and `notPresent`. Whenever using one of these tags, it is necessary to specify a value to be compared as well as what object is being used. This object would be one of the following:

*cookie, header, parameter, property,* or *name.* So, for example, if we wanted to check what type of browser our client is running and then display it only if it is IE 5.5 on Windows 2000, we can do this with the following code snippet:

```
<logic:equal value="Mozilla/4.0 (compatible; MSIE 5.5; Windows NT 5.0)"
             header="User-Agent">
        <bean:header id="browsertype" name="User-Agent"/>
        <b>Your browser User-Agent type is :
             <b><bean:write name="browsertype" ignore="true" />
</logic:equal>
```

Obviously, you can see that this can be quite useful for keeping pages cleaner in browser-dependent code. This is just one example of using a type of value comparison. We used a header example, but if you do a comparison against a property, the variable to be compared with value is the property of the Bean specified by the name attribute. Again, it's possible to do property references as simple, nested, or indexed, or any combination. Using the scope attribute, the scope for the Bean to be searched can be specified. This includes your standard JSP scopes—page, request, session, application, as well as the default, "any scope."

### 8.5.2 Substring Matching

There are two tags, <match> and <notMatch>, that can be used for substring matching in the logic library. These two tags take the same arguments as the sample in the value comparison tags. This means you can substring items specified by cookie, header, parameter, property, and name. There is also an attribute called location that specifies where to match in the string. Possible values for the location attribute are "start" to be matched at the beginning of the string, or "end" if the substring will be matched until the end of the string. An example of using this tag is if you wanted to put a status message on a page. You could pass a parameter to the JSP and then use the substring tag as follows:

```
<logic:match  parameter="type" value="Search" location="start">
  Searching....
</logic:match>
```

Another, more complicated example is that if there is a property value of interest in a Bean that is being used on a JSP, we can match (or notMatch) the value of the property and then do the necessary actions. The following code snippet shows this by searching the property myValue to the end of the string for the value "Test":

```
<logic:notMatch name="myBean" property="myValue" location="end" value="Test">
        ...do appropriate presentation here...
</logic:notMatch>
```

### 8.5.3 Presentation Location

Presentation location has to do with determining how one page gets to another. Basically, this comes down to whether a forward or redirect should be done. The <logic:redirect> tag will send a redirect to the client's browser. This includes URL rewriting if the container supports it. This is done using the `HttpServletResponse encodeRedirectURL()` method and includes the session ID in the URL. URL rewriting is one technique for saving state information between pages. The information is stored as part of the URL as additional parameters. URL rewriting is sometimes used for session management. This is a similar concept to saving information in cookies. URL rewriting is sometimes used when a browser has cookies turned off. The downside of using URL rewriting is that if a user bookmarks a link that was pointed to by a URL rewrite, the link will not be valid later when the session expires.

The base URL is determined by having at least one of the following attributes specified:

- *forward.* Name of an `ActionForward` defined in the `<global-forwards>` section in the `struts-config.xml`, and use the appropriate context as specified.
- *href.* Defined URL argument, used unchanged except for possible URL writing for the session ID.
- *page.* Uses value as an application-relative URI and generates a server-relative URI by including the context path and application prefix. This also allows for the ability to dynamically add query parameters to the generated URL.

So we might have `<logic:redirect forward="success"/>`, which uses the logical forward name from our sample application and then forwards us to the `mainMenu.jsp` as specified in our `<global-forwards>` definition, and `<logic:redirect page="/mainMenu.jsp"/>`, which redirects us using the context-relative path of our `mainMenu.jsp`.

When using the `<logic:forward>` tag, a global action forward is specified. The forward tag has one attribute called `name`, which is the logical name of the `ActionForward`. You can specify whether the specific global forward redirects or forwards when executed by using the `redirect` attribute in the `struts-config.xml file`. We talked about this in Chapter 2. The processing in this tag is identical to that performed by the Struts Controller Servlet when an ActionForward is processed from an Action class return.

A simple sample is `<logic:forward name="logon"/>`.

## 8.5.4 Collection Manipulation

The last area of the Struts-logic library tags we'll examine are those used for manipulating collections. In fact, this is really only one tag, the `<logic:iterate>` tag. The iterate tag is used for executing its body content once for every element inside the specified collection. The only required attribute is `id`, which is the name of a page scope JSP Bean that contains the current element of the collection on each iteration. There are, however, quite a number of optional attributes to give you more control over which collection to use and how to iterate over it. Table 8.4 describes each attribute and its purpose.

When using the `<logic:iterate>` tag, the collection must be one of the following Objects or the iteration will not take place:

- An array of Java objects, including primitive types in 1.1.
- An implementation of `java.util.Collection`, including `ArrayList` and `Vector`.

**Table 8.4:** Attributes of <logic:iterate> tag.

| Attribute | Description |
|---|---|
| collection | A runtime expression that evaluates to a collection object that will be iterated. |
| length | The number of iterations to perform on the collection. This is either an integer value or the name of a JSP Bean in any defined scope of type `java.lang.Integer` that defines the value. If the length is not present, there will be no limit on the number of iterations performed. |
| indexId | The name of a page scope JSP Bean that will contain the current index of the collection on each iteration. |
| name | The name of the JSP Bean containing the collection to be iterated. This is used if the property attribute is not specified. If there is a property attribute, the name plus the property of the Bean are used to call the getter method on the property to return a collection. |
| offset | The zero-relative index of the starting point at which entries from the underlying collection will be iterated through. If not present, the collection will be iterated from the beginning. |
| property | Name of the property, of the JSP Bean specified by name, whose getter returns the collection to be iterated. |
| scope | The standard JSP scopes (page, request, session, application) to search for the Bean named by the name property. The default is "any scope" if not specified. |
| type | Fully qualified Java class name of the element to be exposed through the JSP Bean named from the `id` attribute. If not present, no type conversions will be performed. |

- An implementation of `java.util.Enumeration`.
- An implementation of `java.util.Iterator`.
- An implementation of `java.util.Map`, including `HashMap`, `Hashtable`, and `TreeMap`.

A `Map` is treated slightly differently because the exposed object is actually of type `Map.Entry`. A `Map.Entry` has two properties: a key that is the item is stored in the `Map`, and a value that corresponds to the specified key. For checking collections that can contain `null` values, you can use the `<logic:present>` and `<logic:notPresent>` tags to check for the `Page scope` attribute specified by the `id` attribute. In the case of a `null` value, no attribute will be present for that loop iteration. This prevents having a runtime exception thrown if you try to access a null value. The `<logic:iterate>` tag is a perfect example of a tag that will more than likely be deprecated in favor of the iterate tag provided in JSTL in the near future. One of the reasons for this is that as application container vendors supply implementations for the JSTL, I suspect we will see performance optimizations for things like iterating over collections that will make it worthwhile to use the JSTL tags.

When specifying a `type` attribute, the actual elements of the collection must be assignment compatible with this class or else a request time `ClassCastException` will be thrown.

Let's look at a sample using the <logic:iterate> tag. Assume we create a Bean in our JSP for demonstration. This Bean could actually exist because an Action has placed it in the appropriate scope. It might include results of some business logic that took place in the Action. For the purposes of this sample, we'll just define an ArrayList and save it as a Bean called "list" in our JSP page.

```
<%
  {
    java.util.ArrayList list = new java.util.ArrayList();
    list.add("Item1");
    list.add("Item2");
    list.add("Item3");
    list.add("Item4");
    pageContext.setAttribute("list", list, PageContext.PAGE_SCOPE);

  }
%>
```

Now we can iterate over the ArrayList by referencing the Bean by the name we assigned to it: "list." We set our indexId to be the value of a Bean called "index" so that we can access the current index value in the iteration. We check for the presence of the Bean item in each iteration so that if we had a null value in our array, we can just skip over it.

```
<logic:iterate id="item" name="list" indexId="index">
<logic:present name="item">
  <bean:write name="item"/> [<bean:write name="index"/>]
</logic:present>
</logic:iterate>
```

This iteration produces the following:

```
Item1 [0]
Item2 [1]
Item3 [2]
Item4 [3]
```

The samples included in the CD Manager application demonstrate a number of ways to use the iteration tag that you can use for further reference. As I'm sure you can see, there are many uses for iterations in a JSP, for example, when traversing through result sets, listing items, and producing links. The types of usages go on and will be left to your creativity. For other, more complicated examples and uses of the iteration tag, check out the contrib folder included on the Struts download. There are a number of project references that use the <logic:iterate> tag that could prove helpful to you.

## 8.6 Using the Struts-nested Tag Library

The whole point of having nested tags is so the tags can relate to each other and describe the structure of the model they're managing. The assumptions made by the tags simplify the necessary coding. Using nested tags allows for Beans to be nested. What this means is that one Bean can hold a reference to another Bean. The Bean that *holds* the reference is called the parent. The Bean that *is* the reference is called the child. The properties of parent tags define the nested property for the child tags' properties. If you are a Struts 1.0 developer, you are probably breathing a sigh of relief knowing that you won't have to mangle code any longer to render a display of a list within a list.

The Struts-nested tag library was introduced in Struts 1.1. You are already familiar with almost all the tags in this library since they extend the base Struts tags that we've already talked about. This includes tags from the Html and Logic libraries, except when they are prefixed with a nested namespace. So, for example, if we are nesting an `<html:link>` tag, we would use `<nested:link>` instead. There are also tags new to the Struts-nested tag library. The new tags include `<nested:root>` and `<nested:nest>`. The `<nested:root>` is used to indicate that you are starting a nested scope. This tag is used if `<html:form>` is not being used. The `<html:form>` (for backward compatibility) or `<nested:form>` tags will automatically start a scope for you.

The `<nested:nest>` represents a nesting level for additional markup so that the hierarchy is defined. The `<nested:nest>` and the `<nested:iterate>` are the only two tags in the library that affect the hierarchy. Other tags act either as parent tags or as base tags. A parent tag doesn't affect the hierarchy but can have body content. A base tag has no body content. Examples of parent tags include those related to logic, such as `<nested:empty>` and `<nested:notEmpty>`, as well as the various comparison tags such as `<nested:equals>`, `<nested:greaterThan>`, or `<nested:present>`. Examples of base tags include `<nested:text>`, `<nested:image>`, and `<nested:link>`.

The difference between using non-nested tags and tags from the Struts-nested library is that using the nested version allows the tags to relate to each other in a nested hierarchy. The fundamental logic of the original tags doesn't change, except that all references to Beans and Bean properties will be managed in a nested context using the dot notation that we have already seen when using properties. When building complex pages, it is highly likely that you will want to use the nested features. This makes pages much easier to write and maintain since it allows for the logical flow to be maintained without having to do workarounds, as was required before the 1.1 release.

When dealing with parent and child tags, there must be a getter defined in the parent Bean so that it can provide a reference to the child Bean for access. For example, `public ChildBean getChild()` will return `ChildBean`. This getter requirement is true for all nested properties' methods. So when Struts needs to get or set a property in the child Bean, it will call this method `getChild()` when it gets a reference to the `ChildBean`, and from which it can invoke the appropriate property methods.

Tags can play either a parent role or a child role depending on how they are being used in the situation. The topmost parent in the hierarchy is called the root. The properties of parent tags define the nested property for the child tags' properties. Think of this as you might think

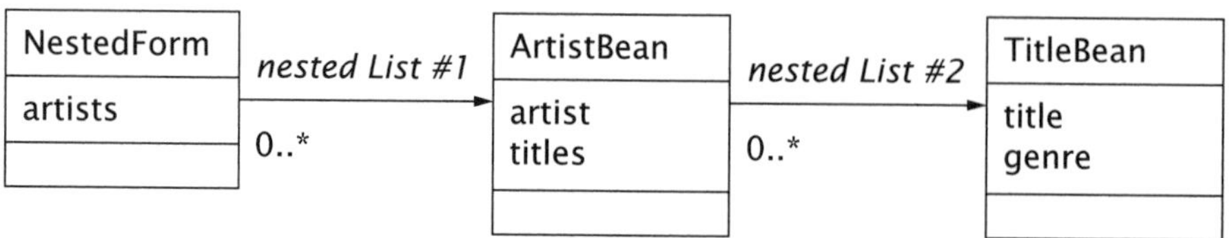


**Figure 8.2:** Nested list diagram.

of inheritance. The child inherits from the parent. Because of the fact that tags can be either a parent or a child, there must be a way to tell when a tag is meant to be a parent and when it's not part of the hierarchy. This quandary is solved by having two separate categories within the Nested library, parent and nonparent.

If a tag implements `org.apache.struts.taglib.nested.NestedParentSupport`, it may be used in a hierarchy as a parent tag. All other tags that are meant to be treated as just markup elements (as in the case of a select list) but not as a nested parent will be skipped in the hierarchy. The root tag specifies the Bean at the top of the hierarchy.

Using nested tags makes your pages much simpler. In fact, it makes it possible to do some pretty sophisticated rendering of lists within lists with just a couple of lines of JSP code. Let's walk through a sample using the structure of our nested lists as shown in Figure 8.2.

Our sample application allows for displaying all the CDs in the database both with and without nested tags, and what we're looking at is the `displayNested.jsp` code. We will go through this line by line.

First, we make use of a custom tag that is specific to our application called `<app:display>`. The attribute is used because we reuse this tag for both nested and non-nested display by setting the `useNestedForm` to "true" or "false," respectively.

```
<app:display useNestedForm="true" />
```

Using this tag provides the mechanism for opening a connection to the database, making a query, and iterating through a result set to place each row of information in the appropriate Bean. That's quite a lot of work accomplished by a one-liner. Granted, in a more structured, enterprise-worthy application, you would want Data Access Objects (DAO) defined to handle your database interaction. But again, this application is for demonstrating how to implement various tasks. Where those tasks actually live is up to the designer.

It is important at this point to mention how the Beans are set up so that you understand how it's possible to use the `<nested:iterate>` tag. For complete code details, view the `cdmanager.forms.beans` package in the sample application. The abbreviated version is as follows. There is a parent Bean called `ArtistBean`. This Bean holds an `artist` property as well as an `ArrayList` of titles. This `ArrayList` is composed of child Beans called `TitleBean`. Each `TitleBean` holds a `title` and `genre` property. As we mentioned, each parent must have a way to get all its children. Our `ArtistBean` has a public method called `getTitles()` that returns all the objects in the `ArrayList`.

Now we can look at the nested calls. We must indicate that we are at the root of a nested hierarchy. It is possible to use either the `<nested:root>` or the `<nested:form>` tag.

```
<nested:form action="/nested">
    <br>
```

Next, we start to iterate through our result set. Here is where the Beans come in. The ArtistBean is already in our session because we had defined access to the nestedForm. The nestedForm has a reference to an ArrayList of ArtistBeans. This action is defined in the web.xml file, and it looks like other actions that we have already defined.

```
<action     path="/nested"
            type="cdmanager.actions.DisplayAllAction"
            name="nestedForm"
            scope="session"
            input="/mainMenu.jsp">
  <forward name="success" path="/displayNested.jsp"/>
</action>
```

So we are back to actually starting the iteration. The beauty of the nested tags is that they hide all these details from the JSP and make it quite easy to implement lists of lists. Before this, such implementation was a real pain to accomplish. So let's keep going.

In the first scope, we are accessing the property artists in the nestedForm. This is actually a list.

```
<nested:iterate property="artists">
```

We access the artist property of each ArtistBean.

```
Artist: <nested:text property="artist" />
```

There are a number of titles associated with each artist, so we begin to iterate through each title by going one step further in the hierarchy. Now we are in the TitleBean.

```
<nested:iterate property="titles">
```

Each TitleBean has a title and genre property. Notice that the properties are relative to the current scope of the nest.

```
<table cellpadding="2" cellspacing="0" border="1">
 <tr>
 <td bgcolor="#008080"><b>Title:</b> <nested:text property="title" /></td>
 <td bgcolor="#008080"><b>Genre:</b> <nested:text property="genre" /></td>
 </tr>
</table>
<br>
```

We are sure to close out each of our nested scopes.

```
        </nested:iterate>
  </nested:iterate>
```

And finally, we put an end to our hierarchy root.

```
</nested:form>
```

You can see from walking through this example that once you have your Beans set up, it is fairly painless to implement an otherwise rather complicated display of doing nested list iterations.

## 8.7 Using the Struts-template Tags

The tags provided in the Struts-template tag library are useful when you have dynamic JSPs that require a common format. Using the Struts-template tags allows for a convenient way to handle working within a given format. It also makes it fairly painless to make layout changes to applications when you are deep into a project and all of a sudden the GUI layout changes. The Struts-template tags have remained the same between Struts 1.0.x and 1.1. Using Struts templating (or most templating for that matter) falls into the implementation details of the Composite View design pattern. This presentation-tier pattern is used to create aggregate Views from atomic subcomponents. Think of these subcomponents as the building blocks all of us engineers played with when we were little. We would use those blocks and assemble them to create great skyscrapers, or at least what appeared to be skyscrapers to five year olds, by placing them one on top of the other. When using the Composite View pattern, each portion of a template can be included dynamically into the final page, but the page layout is managed separately from the content.

There are three tags that work together. They are listed in Table 8.5. These tags work in concert with one another. The attributes associated with each are straightforward. `<template:get>` requires the name of the content to be inserted. The value of the name must match the `name` property used in the put tag. The get tag is used within a template file to determine where the content specified must be inserted. The `<template:insert>` takes the name of the template file as its `name` attribute. It uses what the `<template:put>` tag specifies in its `content` attribute as what will be inserted into the template. However, the layout itself is determined by where the `<template:get>` tags are placed in the template file. Using the `direct` attribute (which is optional) of `<template:put>` determines whether the content should be included or printed to the `JspWriter`. By default, the content is included.

The best way to understand how templates work together is to see them in action. So let's go through a sample.

**Table 8.5:** Template tag reference.

| Tag | Purpose |
|---|---|
| `<template:get>` | Gets content from the request scope and either includes the content or prints it |
| `<template:insert>` | Includes a template into the JSP |
| `<template:put>` | Puts content into request scope |

First, we create a template file. We'll call this file something original like `template.jsp`. This is the template used throughout the application. Think of the template file as the shell, or outline, for how your pages will be presented. The `template.jsp` looks like

```
<%@ include file="taglibs.jsp" %>
<html:html locale="true">

<head>

<title><template:get name='title'/></title>
</head>
<body background='white'>
<table>
    <tr valign='top'>
        <td>
            <table>
                <tr>
                <td><template:get name='header'/></td>
                </tr>
                <tr>
                <td>
                <html:errors/>
                <template:get name='content'/></td>
                </tr>
                <tr>
                <td><template:get name='footer'/></td>
                </tr>
            </table>
        </td>
    </tr>
</table>
</body>
</html:html>
```

Basically, we are defining how the table structure will look and where each portion of the page will live in it. We include our `taglibs.jsp` file because we must be able to resolve the various Struts tags that we are using. Then we define exactly what our layout will look like.

We are defining four request variables. In essence, these are the parameters of the template. Each specific page defines its own content to be included in the template. Remember that the names used in the `<template:get>` must match those used in the `<template:put>`.

Now that we have our layout defined, let's see how to use it within pages.

## 8.7.1 Creating Pages with Template Structure

We separate each page to be displayed into two logical units. One unit is what I like to call the page shell, where we define the files to be included for this page. The other is the actual page content. In essence, the part that usually changes between pages is the content. But it should be noted that you have the ability to change the actual values of the headers or footers or whatever you've defined in your template on a page basis.

For example, say on most pages you want to have a copyright statement as your footer but on one page, you want a privacy statement as well. The layout of the page will be consistent with all the others in the application, but the content of the footer on that one page might be different. If we look at our `login.jsp`, we find the following code:

```
<%@ include file="taglibs.jsp" %>
<template:insert template='/template.jsp'>
  <template:put name='title' content='CD Manager Logon' direct='true'/>
  <template:put name='header' content='/header.jsp' />
  <template:put name='content' content='/logonContent.jsp'/>
  <template:put name='footer' content='/footer.jsp' />
</template:insert>
```

What's being done is that we are applying the `template.jsp` that we defined earlier. In doing so, we are specifying the four areas of our template that are basically parameterized. Demonstrating the use of the `direct` attribute, we are specifying the title to be printed into the file. We use a standard header and footer that we defined. The content is specific to this particular page and specified as the `logonContent.jsp`. Each page will more than likely have specific content to include. You can view the file in more detail from the sample application download.

There's a quick point to make about the title shown in the example. It would be preferable to have something like

```
<template:put name='title' content='<bean:message key="logon.title" />'
          direct='true'/>
```

However, doing so will not work because what will be rendered at runtime is not the message but the printing of "<bean:message key="logon.title" />" on the page without parsing the tag. The reason for this is that you can't use a JSP tag as the value of another JSP tag's attribute. You must use a JSP expression instead. So to do this correctly, use a Utility class to get the message from the resource file.

```
<template:put name='title' content='<%= Message.getMessage("logon.title") %>'
          direct='true'/>
```

The `header.jsp` and `footer.jsp` for this application are nothing more than the inclusion of image files. We could have used HTML files, but the reason we're not using them is that I wanted to include Struts tags in these files so that the strings for the alternate text for the images could be internationalized.

As you can see, templates have many advantages. If you are working on a large application, templates make it much easier to maintain the look and feel of the application. When changes have to be made, they can be made in one place—basically, just the template file itself—and then the page structure will be correct for all the pages that use it. It's very convenient.

Another use for templates is in applications that have different types of clients, each (or many) of which wants a different page header and/or footer along with a different "skin" (i.e., look and feel) for a page. After logging in, you could get the name of the header and footer JSP for that particular page from the user's profile. As for skinning the page (colors, fonts, etc.), you could include a CSS style sheet directive in the template itself (using the .css filename for the client from the user's profile). While this type of usage is probably a bit more advanced than what is covered in this book, it's thrown in here for you to see different possible uses of templating.

## 8.8 Summary

By now, you should be well on your way to having a good (if not better than good) understanding of the tags that are available in Struts and how to use them.

Five tag libraries are available with Struts 1.1: Struts-html, Struts-bean, Struts-logic, Struts-nested, and Struts-template. Each contains multiple tags. We have talked about, and walked through, a number of examples that detail how to use various tags from each of the tag libraries. There is a good chance that most anything you need to do can be accomplished through the use of existing tags that are either provided with Struts or provided from other sources such as the JSTL or Jakarta Taglibs project.

chapter 9

# Internationalizing Your Struts Application

Internationalization is often called I18N, for the 18 letters between I and N. In the global market of software development, it is entirely possible, and most probable, that the application you write today will be running in other languages tomorrow. This chapter focuses on what must be done to ensure that your Struts applications can easily and quickly be internationalized and localized. If you need a full-blown tutorial on internationalized programs, visit the tutorial at *java.sun.com/docs/books/tutorial/i18n/*.

## 9.1 However You Say It: Hello, Bon Jour, Hola, Ni Hao

In general terms, a locale is a geographic, political, or social region. Usually locale refers to the language support for a particular area. A locale can be specified by a standard lowercase two-letter code. It is also common to specify a country code along with the language. This is done to distinguish various dialects. English (en) spoken in the United States (en_US) is different from English spoken in Great Britain (en_GB). I'd drink to this since I have been to Great Britain and found at times that I had no idea what people were saying to me even though I recognized the words . . . I think. And just so you know, it had nothing to do with the fact that we were in a pub at the time.

Locales are represented by the `java.util.Locale` class.

If your application is internationalized, it means that your program can support multiple locales. Localizing an application is the support for the specifics of a particular locale. We will talk about how to set up and code your application so that you can take advantage of international features for prompts and messages. This includes

- UTF-8
- Locales

- PropertyResourceBundles
- Formatted messages
- MessageResources

## 9.2 UTF-8

Java has always used Unicode character encoding with canonical 2-byte per character encoding. This enables language scripts that require multibyte representation to be processed. Unicode covers the principal languages in the Americas, Europe, the Middle East, Africa, India, Asia, and Pacifica. I believe that covers just about everyone, at least on this planet.

Unicode Transformation Format (UTF-8) is used to represent character values in 1 to 4 bytes. This is a better performance encoding than using straight Unicode since most characters will be ASCII characters and therefore require only 1 byte. If you want to take your mind off an upcoming and dreaded visit to your dentist, you can read more details about UTF-8 at *www.unicode.org*. Doing so will surely cure even the worst case of dental phobia.

Character encoding is handled within Java, so you don't really have to worry about it. The reason I mention UTF-8 is that you can set up your application server to encode in UTF-8 if you want to support multiple languages on the same JSP. You can then specify the character set in your JSPs using a META tag like

```
<META HTTP-EQUIV="Content-Type" CONTENT="text/html; charset=UTF-8">
```

Or you can set the http response header directly in the JSP by using the page directive

```
<%@ page contentType="text/html; charset=UTF-8"%>
```

Not all browsers support META tags the same way, so the safer way is to include the directive.

## 9.3 Locales

The `Locale` is used to specify which of the localized language files to use. Each user can have his or her own locale set so that multiple users can all access your application concurrently while viewing it in different languages. Usually the locale is modified in the user's session. By using the Struts tag `<html:html locale="true">` in the JSP, the default locale for that user will be set in the user's session. This value is usually the browser default locale that is indicated by the `Accept-Language` header sent by the browser. It is easy enough to establish the locale setting in whatever browser you use. That way you can force a locale setting so that you can debug for other languages. For example, if we select French as our `Locale` by designating that language in the "language preference" section in our browser configuration, the Logon screen will appear as shown in Figure 9.1. However, if we set our `Locale` to Spanish, our Logon screen appears as in Figure 9.2.

While the images in each screen remain the same in both figures, the text that is displayed in each is correct for the specified locale.

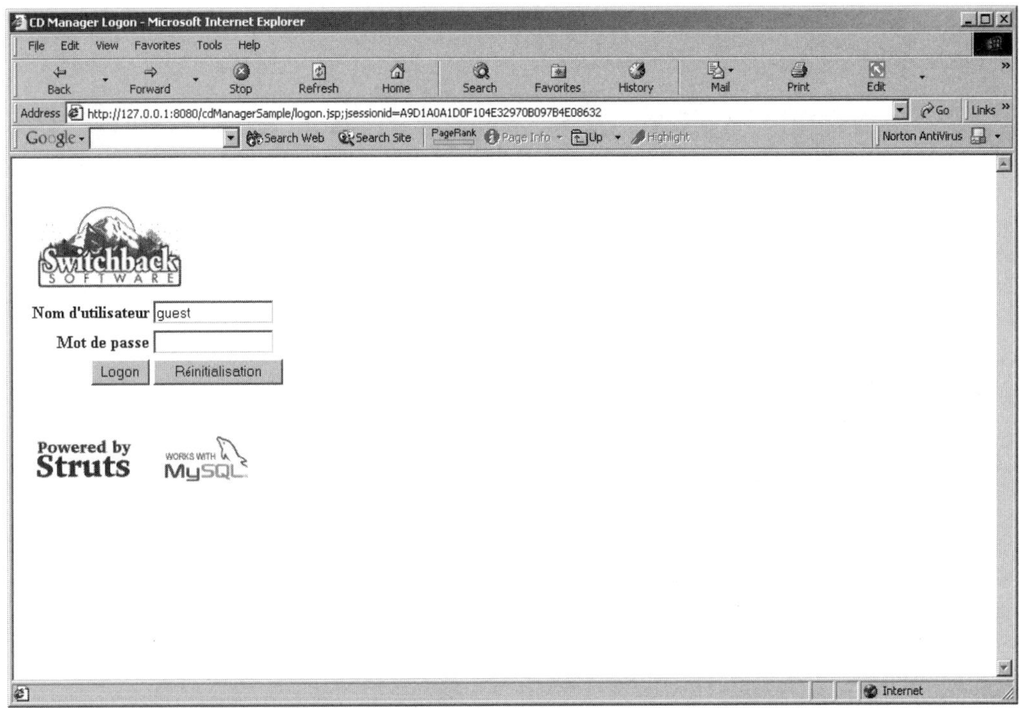


**Figure 9.1:** French Logon screen.

## 9.4 PropertyResourceBundles

`ResourceBundles` are used to hold the text and messages used by your application. The `java.util.ResourceBundle` is an abstract class that allows for subclasses to define localized resources. `PropertyResourceBundle` is a concrete class of `ResourceBundle`. This class allows name/value pairs to be defined in a properties file in the format name=value. This can include button labels or text strings—basically, anything that can be displayed to the user. These resources are stored in a properties file that is specific to the locale. For example, our sample application uses `ApplicationResources.properties` to hold the default key/message pairs. A brief sample of the file is

```
index.logon=Log on to the CD Manager Sample Struts Application
index.title=CD Manager Sample Struts Application
index.heading=Welcome to the CD Manager Sample Struts Application!
logon.title=CD Manager Sample Struts Application-Logon
mainMenu.heading=Main Menu
mainMenu.title=CD Manager Sample Struts Application-Main Menu
mainMenu.logoff=Log Off
```

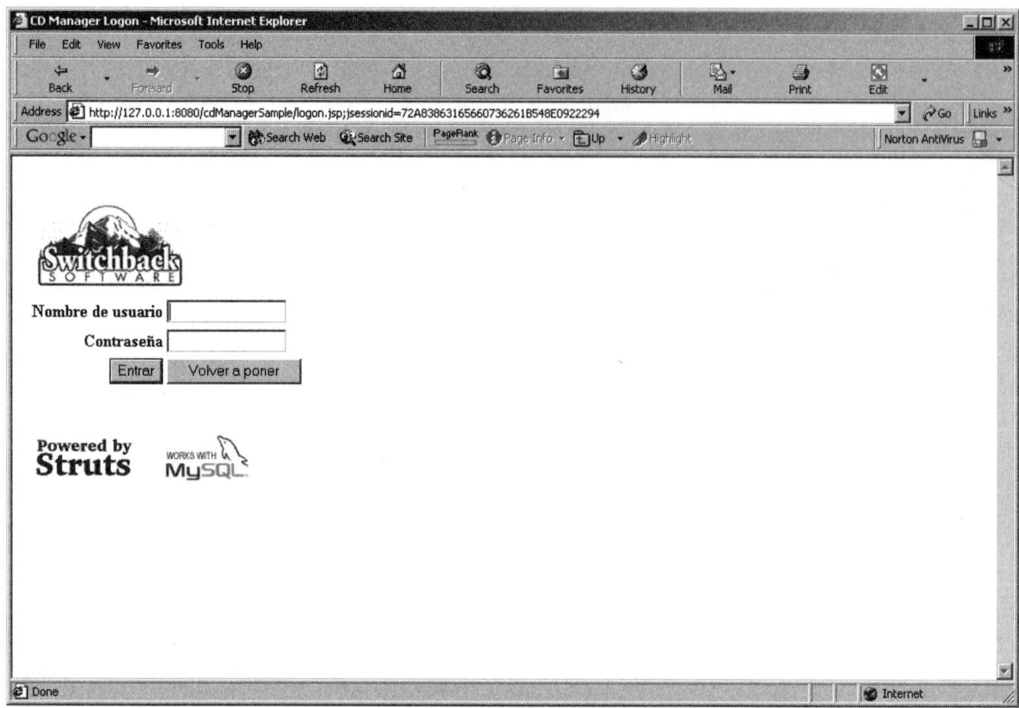


**Figure 9.2:** Spanish Logon screen.

Here we see that each string used in the application has a name, such as `index.logon`, and an associated message. The name (or key) values are what are used by the `<bean:message>` tag to look up a specific key. For example, the `index.jsp` contains

```
<bean:message key="index.title"/>
```

What happens here is that the string "CD Manager Sample Struts Application" is replaced, after the key lookup is done, into the correct file depending on the `Locale` setting that determines the language to be displayed to the user. So if our `Locale` is "es" for Spanish, the string would appear as "Aplicación de CD Manager Sample Struts."

To view the full default resource file, consult the sample application download. For each language that your application supports, you create an appropriately named resource file that has the translated text in it. For example, our sample application also supports Spanish and French, so we have two additional resource files that follow the locale naming conventions. These files are named `ApplicationResources_es.properties` for Spanish, and `ApplicationResources_fr.properties` for French. If you change the default `Locale` in your browser to be either French or Spanish, you will see the appropriate language text. The default `ResourceBundle` for an application is defined in the `struts-config.xml` file for each subapplication as

```
<message-resources parameter="cdmanager.ApplicationResources"/>
```

where the parameter includes the package structure of where your ResourceBundle is located.

The application's message ResourceBundles are loaded by the JVM running Struts and are therefore shared among all the users of a particular Struts web application. The only thing that is unique to a particular user is the java.util.Locale object that indicates the user's preference. This makes it possible for users to actually change Locales on-the-fly and still get the correct language text. This is a great feature for anyone who has ever attempted simultaneous language support in an application.

To convert your localized ApplicationResources.properties to UTF-8, you use the tool named native2ascii. This tool is part of the JDK. This utility takes characters that are non-Latin 1 and non-Unicode and makes them into Unicode-encoded characters. For example, if we had a Greek version (we don't in the sample application), you could run the command:

```
native2ascii -encoding UTF-8 ApplicationProperties_el.properties
ApplicationProperties_el.propertiesNew
```

then you'd rename the file ApplicationProperties_el.properties.

All the internationalized words have been converted to Unicode (UTF-8) standards, and now the browser will be able to read it. See? It's really not Greek after all. It is also possible to use the <native2ascii> preprocess task to run this program directly from your ANT build.xml. That way, you can convert source files maintained in a native operating system encoding to ASCII, prior to compilation. For more information, you can find the various processing tasks for ANT at *jakarta.apache.org/ant/manual/index.html.*

## 9.5 Formatted Messages

While it's possible to have all of your name/value pairs defined in your PropertyResource-Bundles, it is frequently required to allow for parametric replacement within message text. This allows what amounts to a static text string to have dynamic content in it. Parametric replacement is done by simply including an {x} for the parameter number, where *x* is a number value. It is possible to have up to four parameters to a message.

For example, if we look at the name/value pair

```
database.load=Cannot load database from {0}
```

from our ApplicationResources.properties file, we see that the path specifying the database is an argument for the dynamic value. In this example, we are using only one dynamic value. Then it's possible to include the parameter from the ActionForm validation method when creating a new error message like

```
new ActionError("database.load",dbPath);
```

If you were accessing a message that had parameters from a JSP, the tag might look like

```
<bean:message key="database.load" arg0='default location'/>
```

The full set of features supported by formatted messages are documented in the java.text.MessageFormat API Javadocs.

## 9.6 The MessageResources Class

The MessageResource class is part of the org.apache.struts.util package. It provides a mechanism so that you don't have to worry about which ResourceBundle to use. By specifying a Locale, and a message key, the MessageResource will retrieve the correct string for you. From an Action, you can pass the HttpServletRequest parameter to the getResources(request) method call. This will return the message resources for the current subapplication. You can then do a lookup on the specific name you are interested in.

```
MessageResources messages    = getResources(request);
String message = messages.getMessage("myMessage");
```

If you wanted to dynamically set the Locale for a user, you typically do it in an Action.

```
java.util.Locale locale = new java.util.Locale("es");
setLocale(request,locale);
```

This changes the user's default locale (and language) to Spanish. The setLocale method of Action basically just sets a session attribute called Action.LOCALE_KEY (found in the Action class as a static string) to the locale you pass in.

## 9.7 Summary

Overall, there really isn't all that much work to do in order to internationalize your application. Most of the work is just translating the strings in your resource files. The real grunt work is handled under the covers by the Struts framework.

chapter **10**

# Configuring, Testing, and Rolling out Your Application

So, here we are nearing the end. We've gone through all the major components in Struts and we've built all the components necessary for our sample application. I'd like to spend some time now on rolling out your application and reviewing some things to take into account in a production environment.

## 10.1 The WAR File

Web applications are typically built and assembled into web archive (WAR) files. These are basically JAR (Java archive) files that contain all the classes, resource bundles, JSPs, and configuration files necessary for a web container to run your application. Prior to the Servlet API Specification v2.2, there was no set way to define your web application between server platforms. This proved to be problematic in the sense of the "write once, run anywhere" Java mantra, which turned into the "write once, rebuild to fit your web container, run anywhere" Java mantra.

Web servers now accept a WAR in a standard format if they support the Servlet v2.2 specification or later.

A WAR file has an extension of `.war`. WAR files are handled specially by web application containers so that it is extremely easy to deploy web applications. For a more detailed discussion of the WAR format, see the Servlet 2.3 specification at *www.jcp.org/aboutJava/communityprocess/final/jsr053/*.

The top-level directory of your web application hierarchy, also called the document root of your application, is where the HTML files and JSPs are placed. The *context path* is where the application actually lives on the server. So, for example, if the system administrator assigns the application to the context path /cdmanager, then a request URI referring to `/cdmanager/index.html` will retrieve the `index.html` file from that document root.

When Tomcat is started, it automatically expands the WAR file into its unpacked form so that it can be executed. For more information on other options for deploying applications on Tomcat, see *jakarta.apache.org/tomcat/tomcat-4.0-doc/appdev/deployment.html10.*[1]

### 10.1.1 Setting Up the WAR Layout

It makes sense to use the required file structure in your WAR file. If you take a look at the ANT `build.xml` file that accompanies our sample application, you will see that I have a `prepare.dist` target that copies all the files from our development structure into the defined WAR structure to prepare for deployment. The structure is as follows:

- *The document root.* This becomes `cdManagerSample` because that is what our WAR file is called. By default, Tomcat will deploy WAR files under the same name as the WAR file.
- *Client files and images.* The JSPs (and HTML files if there are any), along with other files that must be visible to the client browser (such as JavaScript, stylesheets, and images necessary for the application), are under the document root. Sometimes, depending on how large and complicated your application is, it makes sense to break down a directory structure. For example, you may want to put all JSPs in one directory, all images in another, etc.
- */WEB-INF/web.xml.* The Web Application Deployment Descriptor is the XML file describing the Servlets and other components that make up the application. This is the same `web.xml` file that we discussed in detail in Chapter 6.
- */WEB-INF/classes/.* This directory contains any Java class files and resources required for the application. This can include JAR files of both Servlet and non-Servlet classes. Java package hierarchy structure must be maintained in the class directory; otherwise, you will get `ClassNotFound` exceptions. This is not a problem if you follow the `prepare.dist` target in the provided `build.xml` file.
- */WEB-INF/lib/.* This directory contains JAR files that contain Java class files and resources required by the application, such as third-party class libraries or JDBC drivers. This is where the `Struts.jar` lives.

The files in the `WEB-INF/classes` and `WEB-INF/lib` directories are automatically visible to your web application. There is no need to alter the system CLASSPATH for classes that might be accessed from other parts of your web application if they run in the same context.

While JSPs can reside in the document root, sometimes it makes sense to place them in the `WEB-INF` directory of the application. Most, but not all, web containers provide security for files below the `WEB-INF` directory. Having the files located here prevents direct access from a browser client. What this means is that the pages are only accessed from Actions. Forwards from the `ActionServlet` are allowed by the container. Then the security of the site is moved

[1]The Tomcat "manager" webapp lets you install and remove applications without restarting Tomcat. Also, custom ANT tasks let you integrate these types of commands directly in your build scripts. See a Tomcat 4.1.x test release for details.

from the presentation (i.e., having a security check in the JSP file) to the Controller. The one thing to think about here is this. Your application should rarely if ever have direct access to a JSP. All page accesses should always go through Actions anyway. If this is the case, then the actual JSP name is never exposed to the user anyway, so it is unlikely that a client will access the page directly.

## 10.2 Building to Deploy

When you are ready to test and deploy an application, it is quite easy. I've provided a target in the ANT `build.xml` file with the sample application that is an all-inclusive target. Keep in mind that my `deploy` target is for Tomcat. However, it includes the same steps you need to perform for any other web container; you just might need to tweak a few things like directory names. Take it and modify it to fit the exact needs of your project.

If you type "ant deploy" in the directory of your `build.xml`, the following will happen:

1. Any source files that have changed are compiled.
2. All classes, resource bundles and property files, JSP files, and the `Struts.jar` are copied to fit the structure of the WAR file layout as described in the previous section.
3. The new WAR file is copied into the `webapps` directory.
4. The Tomcat `work` directory is deleted so that Tomcat recompiles any JSP file in the application.

Note: Before doing a deploy, stop Tomcat. Otherwise, the current directory files are in use and can't be overwritten.

When you restart Tomcat, it will recognize the WAR file and expand it so that the context becomes available in the container. Just enter the URL of your Struts application. This would be the same name as the WAR file, minus the `.war` extension.

So in our sample application, you access *127.0.0.1:8080/cdManagerSample* if it was running on your local server with the default Tomcat HTTP port. The IP address 127.0.0.1 can also be referenced as "localhost." The welcome page displayed for the application is determined in the `web.xml` associated with this application, in our case, `index.jsp`. That is the `<welcome-page>` element we talked about earlier in our `web.xml` discussion.

## 10.3 Jar Files

There are a number of JAR files necessary for Struts 1.1. These include the various JARs provided from Jakarta Commons. For the most part, you really don't need to be concerned about them as long as they are available to your application. All the necessary JAR files are included in the Struts distribution. I've added all the appropriate JAR files to the CLASSPATH in the sample application `build.xml` file so that you can see how to build a deployable application. The `Struts.jar` gets a little bit more attention.

### 10.3.1 The Struts.jar File

You may have noticed that the Struts.jar file is added into your application WAR file in the deploy build target. It's necessary to have a copy of the Struts.jar file packaged with each application and not in the CLASSPATH of your application server. It might be tempting to put the Struts.jar in a shared location that isn't necessarily on the CLASSPATH of the application server but is accessible to each web application through a symbolic link, but this won't do. The reason it won't do is a class loader issue.

The classes in the Struts.jar instantiates your Action and Form classes. If the Struts.jar is in the WEB-INF/lib directory of your application, it will find the classes of your application. If the Struts.jar is located somewhere else in the CLASSPATH, then the classes in your web application will not be found by the Struts.jar and you will have ClassNotFound exceptions being thrown.

## 10.4 Using Logging for Debugging

We have all had our share of System.out.println ("Yet Another Log Message") in our code. Inserting log statements into code is an easy and fairly painless way to debug it. While println statements don't fall into the glamorous category, they are a very useful tool for debugging. However, it becomes increasingly difficult to debug multithreaded and distributed applications—logging can help.

Although there can be some drawbacks, like performance hits, to an application, I'm of the opinion that the amount of CPU time spent in log statements at runtime is rarely of great concern in the overall performance of the system. Because logging systems are usually high-performance components, there are likely other areas in your application that are chewing up more CPU time than the log statements are. It is also possible to alter log levels at runtime so that logging messages can be increased or decreased.

Struts 1.1 uses the Jakarta Commons Logging package from the Components Repository. You can find more information on Logging at *jakarta.apache.org/commons/logging.html*. The Logging package provides a wrapper around any logging API that you might choose to use. This is convenient because using the Logging API removes both compile and runtime dependencies on any one Log package. You can then use whatever implementation you like without having to worry about going back and redoing all of your logging statements. Having to do that is a monumental pain.

The Logging package has an intelligent discovery mechanism (the concrete subclass of LogFactory called LogFactoryImpl), and uses the following algorithm to select the logging implementation to instantiate. First, it will try to use a factory configuration attribute named org.apache.commons.logging.Log to identify the requested implementation class. If that isn't available, it will check to see if Log4J *(jakarta.apache.org/log4j/docs/index.html)* is and, if it is, will return an instance of org.apache.commons.logging.impl.Log4JCategoryLog.

If Log4J is not available, it will check to see if the JDK 1.4 is being used and will return an instance of org.apache.commons.logging.impl.Jdk14Logger. JDK 1.4 is the first release to have Logging classes built into it.

If all three of the previous steps fail, then an instance of `org.apache.commons.logging.impl.NoOpLog` is returned. The `NoOpLog` class will be returned, and basically the log messages are just thrown away.

You are able to log according to six log levels.

1. trace (the least serious)
2. debug
3. info
4. warn
5. error
6. fatal (the most serious)

If using Log4J as your implementation, you can also turn logging completely off, or you can log all messages regardless of their level.

This book used Log4J as the logging implementation in our sample program primarily because it's another valuable open source project that deserves credit and because it is widely popular. Log4J can be found at *jakarta.apache.org/log4j/docs/index.html*. One thing to make sure of if you are using Log4J is that your configuration is loaded before your `ActionServlet` is loaded. This is done by initializing Log4J before Struts actually starts. So in the `web.xml` file we have

```
<servlet>
        <servlet-name>log4j-init</servlet-name>

<servlet-class>cdmanager.Log4jInitServlet</servlet-class>
        <init-param>
            <param-name>log4j-init-file</param-name>
            <param-value>/WEB-INF/log4j.properties</param-value>
        </init-param>
        <load-on-startup>1</load-on-startup>
 </servlet>
```

Then the sample servlet (which is also available on the Log4J site) looks like

```
package cdmanager;

import javax.servlet.http.*;
import java.io.PrintWriter;
import java.io.IOException;
import org.apache.log4j.PropertyConfigurator;

public class Log4jInitServlet extends HttpServlet {

     public void init() {
         String prefix = getServletContext().getRealPath("/");
         String file = getInitParameter("log4j-init-file");
```

```
            if (file != null) {
                PropertyConfigurator.configure(prefix+file);
            }
        }
        public void doGet(HttpServletRequest req, HttpServletResponse res) { }
    }
```

Then we include a configuration file that is used by Log4J for setting the log levels, appenders, and patterns to use. This configuration file, `log4j.properties`, is placed in the `WEB-INF` of our application. You can view the `log4j.properties` file in the CD Manager sample application for more details.

Actually writing a message to a log is a matter of having the proper imports in your class, such as

```
import org.apache.commons.logging.Log;
import org.apache.commons.logging.LogFactory;
```

and then creating a Log instance. The instance can be associated with the class by doing the following:

```
private Log log = LogFactory.getLog(this.getClass().getName());
```

Because I have Log4J available on my system, the Log instance I receive is of `org.apache.commons.logging.impl.Log4JCategoryLog` because of the discovery mechanism mentioned earlier. It is simply a matter of deciding when and what you want to log. As a sample in `LogonAction.java`, I have various trace and debug statements. A debug statement to log user and session information looks like

```
if (log.isDebugEnabled()) {
        log.debug("LogonAction: User '" + user.getUserName()
                  + "' logged on in session " + session.getId());
}
```

Since this isn't a Log4J book, I wanted to give you the pieces that are used for logging, how to accomplish logging for debugging, and a taste of how to use logging in our sample application.

## 10.5 Unit Testing

Testing, as well as having a test suite, is an important piece in the overall success of your project. There are many times when I've heard, "I don't have time to write test cases" from engineers. The fact of the matter is, you don't have time *not* to write test cases. Having an available test suite can help identify problems in the code before an application is running in production. It also makes it quick and relatively easy to run regression tests when new features are added to your application.

Testing server-side applications requires some planning in order to test correctly. One of the easiest tools to learn, and biggest bang for the buck (since it's free), is JUnit, an open source project that can be found at *www.junit.org*. Cactus is another Jakarta project that provides server-side unit testing and is built on top of JUnit. Cactus can be found at *jakarta.apache.org/cactus/index.html*. If you are looking for a Struts-specific testing environment, visit *strutstestcase.sourceforge.net*. StrutsTestCase combines support for testing Struts components using either a mock object approach or an in-container approach using the Cactus framework. I'm using JUnit in our sample application just because all the other frameworks are based on it. You can read up more on Cactus or StrutsTestCase to see if those fit your needs better. But they all will look fairly similar in approach to JUnit.

JUnit puts itself into the slightly extreme programming (XP) paradigm. While I really don't want to preach one type of development method over another, writing test cases often and running them often is beneficial, regardless of which method you subscribe to. Though this book isn't about teaching you how to write test cases, I thought that it would be helpful to show you how you can write test cases quickly and easily to test your Struts application.

Test cases should become part of your source tree. As you build, edit, and refine your source code, you should also be updating your test cases. Using JUnit is simple. You create a test class that mimics your package and class files. So we have

```
package cdmanager.actions;
import junit.framework.Test;
import junit.framework.TestCase;
public class TestLogonAction extends TestCase
```

This would be the test case that tests the `LogonAction` in our `cdmanager.actions` package. All the unit tests for `LogonAction` are maintained in `TestLogonAction`. All the tests are collectively known as a suite. A suite is built dynamically by the JUnit framework using Java Reflection. By returning the JUnit Test object from the `suite()` method call, all the methods contained in this class that begin with "test" are added to the suite and are executed. The suite method looks like

```
public static Test suite()
{
    // All methods starting with "test" will be executed in the test suite.
    return new TestSuite(TestLogonAction.class);
}
```

So basically all of your Test classes follow a similar structure, and you just have to keep adding test cases to the file. The suite is executed by the TestRunner program that is provided with JUnit. You can run TestRunner with either a text, AWT, or Swing GUI by simply running the command

```
java junit.swingui.TestRunner cdmanager.actions.TestLogonAction
```

Of course, you need to make sure that your CLASSPATH is set up correctly. You could have included

```
java -cp .\build\classes;.\lib\junit.jar
```

on the command line if you were running the TestRunner from the main directory for the CD Manager application. Following that build structure, the location of your test file classes (`.\build\classes`) as well as the `junit.jar` file are specified so that you can execute your tests.

We won't go into all the details of how to write proper test cases, but a test case sample is included with the CD Manager application, along with a TestRunner script to get you started. Refer to any of the resources listed on *www.junit.org* for more thorough references. And for more details on the various features available in JUnit, visit their website and download the latest version.

## 10.6 Maintaining Your Application

Once an application is built, tested, and deployed, you're done, right? Well, as most of us know, that is rarely the case. One of the success characteristics I consider necessary to determine how well you built a system is how easy it is to maintain. Elegant solutions are those that require the smallest amount of maintenance. This includes how fast a new engineer comes up to speed on an entire application, how quickly requirement changes and enhancements can be made to the existing application, and how long your Objects live before they are bulging at the seams because of poor design decisions.

### 10.6.1 Keeping Up with the Joneses

There are constant improvements being made to the framework and work going on in the development community when you're working with an open source project such as Struts.

A major strength of the Struts framework is that there is a high degree of backward compatibility to previous Struts releases. This plays an important role as more and more production applications roll out using Struts as their MVC framework. It's best to keep up with the mailing list to see what bugs are being fixed and what features are being added.

The Struts framework was the brainchild of Craig R. McClanahan who is also on a number of Java-related expert groups at Sun Microsystems. The experiences of the Struts user community and the features present in Struts that serve the community well for the MVC model mean that many of the Struts features have the potential to influence and possibly become part of the Java standards being worked on as part of the Java Community Process (JCP).

In the same sense, standards have the ability to effect how features get juggled into Struts releases. For example, many of the custom tags available in the JavaServer Pages Standard Tags Library (JSTL) could very well, and should, be used within the Struts framework. You can find more information at *jcp.org/aboutJava/communityprocess/review/jsr052/index.html*.

Another example is the JavaServer Faces (JSF), a proposed standard set of components for user interfaces. This includes handling events, validation, and navigation. JSF is another example of new technology that can, and probably will, play a role in the Struts framework and how it grows. Therefore, as we move forward it might make sense to rev your applications when appropriate so that they are taking advantage of the most current features available. It looks as if there will be an integration library coming soon that lets you use JSF and Struts 1.1

together. Tighter integration between the two will occur in a later version of Struts. Keep up to date on JSF at *jcp.org/jsr/detail/127.jsp*.

Many people follow the "if it ain't broke, don't fix it" model, and that's fine. Sometimes there really is no need to stir the pot if everything is working and the business requirements are being met. However, that doesn't mean that you shouldn't be aware of what the potential of new features and fixes might provide to your development. When using open source, you have access to the source code. So it is entirely possible to just check all the source code for Struts into your own development source control system and never have to touch it again. But the reality of it is this. We are all developers and we're always looking for ways to improve our applications and our skills. Keeping an eye on what's coming down the pike is part of our nature.

## 10.7 Summary

Chapter 10 covered how to take an application that has been built, package it up into a WAR file so that it can be deployed, and then deploy it. We also looked at some common tasks such as logging and unit testing and how to use them effectively. In addition, we also talked about maintaining your application for the future.

As a final thought, there are a couple of projects taking place that could easily come into radar view concerning Struts. The JSP Standard Tag Library as well as JavaServer Faces are projects to keep an eye on in the future.

chapter 11

# Additional Useful Struts Packages and Extensions

In the preface of this book, I defined the 80%/20% rule that was used to determine what was—and what wasn't—relevant for inclusion in this book. While we've certainly covered lots of useful features, I wanted to give you a feeling for some of the items that might fall into the 20% part of the rule. Though there's not a great deal of detail about how to use some of these more advanced features, it's presented as a sort of primer so that as you progress into more sophisticated application development, you will have an understanding of what else is available. Let's start with Tiles.

## 11.1 Tiles

Tiles (formerly known as Components) is a framework added into the Struts 1.1 release under the `contrib` folder. Tiles is completely focused on the V in MVC. Tiles is a more sophisticated template engine than that provided in the Struts-template tag library. It is another example of an implementation of the Composite View pattern that we talked about in the Struts-template tag library. With Tiles you can do such things as

- Screen definitions that include inheritance
- Templating
- Layouts for common pages, menus, and portals
- Dynamic page building
- Reuse tiles
- I18N support for locale-specific loading
- Multichannels that allow for loading of tiles dependent on a key stored in the JSP session

Basically, you define Tiles (or sections) of your pages as we did in the template example. There might be a Tile for each section like title, header, content, and footer. The Tiles are then assembled together to form a template. There is a library of common layouts that you can look through located in the `tiles/web/layouts` directory. Because there is a strong resemblance to the Struts-template tags, sometimes it is common to define the namespace of a template to the `tiles.tld`. So the tag `<template:put>` might actually be referencing the custom tag defined in the `tiles.tld` file.

Tiles are useful when building complicated web applications like portals or when trying to do things such as layering titles vertically on top of one another. Tiles also use definitions that are defined in an XML description file. This allows for a high degree of flexibility in terms of screen definitions, centralized declarations, parameters, and other features. While an entire chapter could be written on Tiles, it's not in this book because it exceeds the 80% rule. I suggest that if it is something that sounds like it would be useful to your project, you explore it in more detail at *www.lifl.fr/˜dumoulin/tiles/index.html*.

## 11.2 Validator

The Validation framework is now part of the Struts package structure and can be found in `org.apache.struts.validator`. Why use the Validator framework? The answer is that Validator makes life a bit easier when you have to deal with required fields, determining matches to a regular expression, email, credit card, and date validation as well as server-side type checking.

This framework is based on the Commons Validator that can be found at *jakarta.apache.org/commons*. The purpose is to perform server-side validations based on validation rules located in the `validation.xml`. It is possible to add custom validations to this file. Rules can be defined for different locales. It's possible to store your specific validator rules in a separate file. This is accomplished by setting the `config-rules` parameter in the `ValidatorServlet` contained in the `web.xml` file. The standard file is available in the Struts dist directory and is called `validator-rules.xml`.

Using this framework requires adding the `ValidatorServlet` to your `web.xml` file with its appropriate configuration parameters and then extending `org.apache.struts.validator.action.ValidatorForm` instead of `org.apache.struts.action.ActionForm`.

Validator is the first component to implement the new PlugIn interface in Struts 1.1. By supporting the `init()` and `destroy()` methods of PlugIn, the `ValidatorPlugin` is notified about application startup and shutdown events without having to be concerned with extending `ActionServlet` code. Plugins are configured in the `struts-config.xml` file by setting the `<plug-in>` element. The example using Validator is

```
<plug-in className="org.apache.struts.validator.ValidatorPlugIn">
  <set-property property="pathname" value="/WEB-INF/validator-rules.xml"/>
  <set-property property="pathname" value="/WEB-INF/validation.xml"/>
</plug-in>
```

You can also add pluggable validators by adding a validation method signature to your `ValidatorAction` class. For more details, reference the `org.apache.struts.validator.util.StrutsValidator` class.

## 11.3 Uploading Files

Sometimes it is necessary to provide file uploads from a client to the server. Fortunately, the grunt work was taken out of this task thanks to the `org.apache.struts.upload` package. This package is helpful in dealing with multipart data and includes a number of classes to handle various situations. Classes include

- `BufferedMultipartInputStream`, which implements buffering for an `InputStream` as well as providing a reliable `readLine` method
- `DiskMultipartRequestHandler`, which is a `MultipartRequestHandler` that writes file data directly to temporary files on disk
- `MultipartIterator`, which allows for reading the input data of a multipart request and splitting it up into input elements

## 11.4 Commons Utilities

The Struts utilities package offers several families of classes to help solve those problems that pop up over and over when building web applications. Most of the classes in this package do not rely on the controller Servlet framework or the custom tag libraries, so they can be used in general Java application programming. Because many of the Classes were so useful, as of Struts 1.1, they were moved into the Jakarta Commons project. These include the Bean Utilities, Collections, and Digester packages. We talked about the Logging packages and how to use them in the previous chapter, so I won't go into it again here, but just note that the Logging provided in Struts actually comes from the Commons project.

### 11.4.1 Bean Utilities

`org.apache.commons.beanutils` components provide wrappers around the Java Reflection and Introspection APIs. By using classes in the `beanutils` package, it is possible to access getter and setter methods dynamically without compiled-in knowledge of the method names. These classes are used with the custom tag libraries of Struts, so it makes sense that if you are writing additional custom tags for your application, you might want to look further into what is available in this package. Brief descriptions of the available classes at the time of this writing are listed in Table 11.1.

### 11.4.2 Collection Utilities

The collections and comparator utility packages offer a plethora of classes that build upon the extensive collections support introduced in the JDK 1.2. The functionality provided in these packages is broken down into the following implementation categories:

- List
- Map
- Stack and queue

**Table 11.1:** Classes available in commons Beanutils package.

| Class | Description |
| --- | --- |
| `BeanUtils` | Populates JavaBeans properties via reflection |
| `ConvertUtils` | Converts string values to objects of the specified class |
| `MappedPropertyDescriptor` | Describes one mapped property |
| `MethodUtils` | Focuses on methods in general rather than properties in particular |
| `PropertyUtils` | Uses Java Reflection APIs to allow for generic property getter and setter operations |

- Bag interface and implementations
- Adaptors
- Utilities
- Transformation tools

There are 35 classes available, so they're not all included in these pages. Suffice it to say that it is worth the cup of coffee to peruse the available Javadocs to get familiar with what these classes provide. Many of these classes can be directly applied to your server-side web application development.

### 11.4.3 Digester

The `digester` package provides rules-based processing of XML documents. This is great for reading configuration files so that Objects can be initialized correctly. What makes this package useful is that you can do many of the things fairly simply that would otherwise require more in-depth knowledge of DOM or SAX processing. This is accomplished by having a Java object-mapping module that allows specifying rules when patterns in the XML are recognized.

There are existing rules provided, and it is also easy to add your own. The `digester` package is used in our sample application in the `DatabaseServlet` to read the configuration database file. The following code enables us to create a new `Digester` object, set some configuration settings on the `Digester` itself, and then create a `User` object specific to our application that the `Digester` sets the properties in based on the element values in the XML file. As demonstrated by the use of the `CdInfo` object, this is used for nested elements as well. The input stream is then parsed, and the XML to Objects mapping is completed with the appropriate values. The lines of code to accomplish this are

```
BufferedInputStream bis = new BufferedInputStream(is);
Digester digester = new Digester();
digester.push(this);
digester.setDebug(debug);
```

```
digester.setValidating(false);
digester.addObjectCreate("database/user", "cdmanager.User");
digester.addSetProperties("database/user");
digester.addSetNext("database/user", "addUser");
digester.addObjectCreate("database/user/cd", "cdmanager.CdInfo");
digester.addSetProperties("database/user/cd");
digester.addSetTop("database/user/cd", "setOwner");

digester.parse(bis);
bis.close();
```

This code is incredibly simpler, I can assure you, than setting up and parsing the XML using either DOM or SAX.

A number of advanced features are available when using a `Digester`. These include the ability to plug in your own pattern-matching engine, namespace-aware processing, and the creation of `RuleSets` that encapsulate rules to be used in multiple applications. If you are explicitly reading in any XML files into your applications and need to map them to the appropriate Java Objects, the `Digester` is worth a look.

## 11.5 Workflow

In our sample application, we went through an example of how to create and use a wizard. A wizard is a simple example of a workflow where there are Actions that must be completed given certain conditions and in a certain order.

The workflow extension takes the notion of a state machine, which is basically what a workflow is, and creates a framework around how to implement it. This extension can be found in the Struts `contrib` folder. It is possible for workflows to be linear or branch, or to replace other workflows. It really depends on what your business requirements are.

There are ways to identify what the previous, current, and next state should be in a workflow, as well as how to determine primary and secondary workflows. This is done by setting properties in the action defined in the `struts-config.xml`. If there is no previous or next state, then the workflow ends and information that has been stored during the workflow is acted upon or thrown away. Since a workflow spans multiple actions (like our wizard), any attributes that were stored are automatically cleaned up when the workflow ends. There can be any number of `IworkFlowCleanupAction` instances in the workflow context. Each instance has its cleanup methods called when the workflow is completed. For more information, check out the site at *www.livinglogic.de/Struts/*.

## 11.6 Other Items of Interest

There is an ever-growing list of new extensions and tools becoming available for the Struts framework. I'm sure that there will be new ones added by the time you read this. It is best to frequently check the resources link on the Struts home page to keep abreast of the latest developments. However, there are a few that are worthwhile to point out here. You can investigate on your own to see if there are any you can make use of.

In the Struts `contrib` folder, there is the Scaffold framework written by Ted Husted. Scaffold included many useful samples and utilities that you can incorporate into your applications. The Artimus Project (also written by Ted) is a news poster application that provides another useful sample to walk through.

Expresso is another framework that integrates with Struts (as of Expresso 4.0) and adds database-specific capabilities. Basically, it is a library of components that provides common features used by web applications. If you need to build highly functional database applications, it is a good place to start. Expresso provides such features as database-stored security, object relational mapping, background job handling and scheduling, automated table manipulation, database connection pooling, email connectivity, event notification, and caching, to rattle off a few features. You can find Expresso details at *www.jcorporate.com*

## 11.7 Summary

There are a number of very useful extensions and packages that can be used in, or with, the Struts framework. As you build more complicated and sophisticated applications, the power of these extensions and packages will become more apparent.

## 11.8 Closing Thoughts

Congratulations! We have designed, built, debugged, tested, and deployed an application using Struts 1.1. You now have the power to move forward and tackle some of the complicated applications waiting to be built and do it faster than your co-workers who don't know Struts.

Keep yourself up to date on what becomes available in the Struts world. There certainly will be new and exciting features that will help us all. In fact, as you build your application, if there are features you create that help you, they will probably help others. Give back to the Struts community and consider incorporating your brainstorms into the Struts project code.

I hope that this book has increased your knowledge, decreased your ramp-up time, and captured your attention insofar as the power of the Struts framework is concerned. Now go put it all to good use and build yourself some cool applications.

appendix A

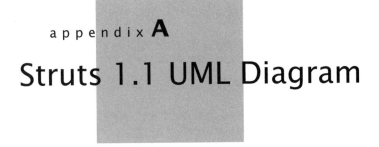

# Struts 1.1 UML Diagram

Figure A.1 shows a complete UML diagram of the Struts 1.1 architecture. If you are not familiar with UML notation, read through the resources provided in Appendix B concerning UML.

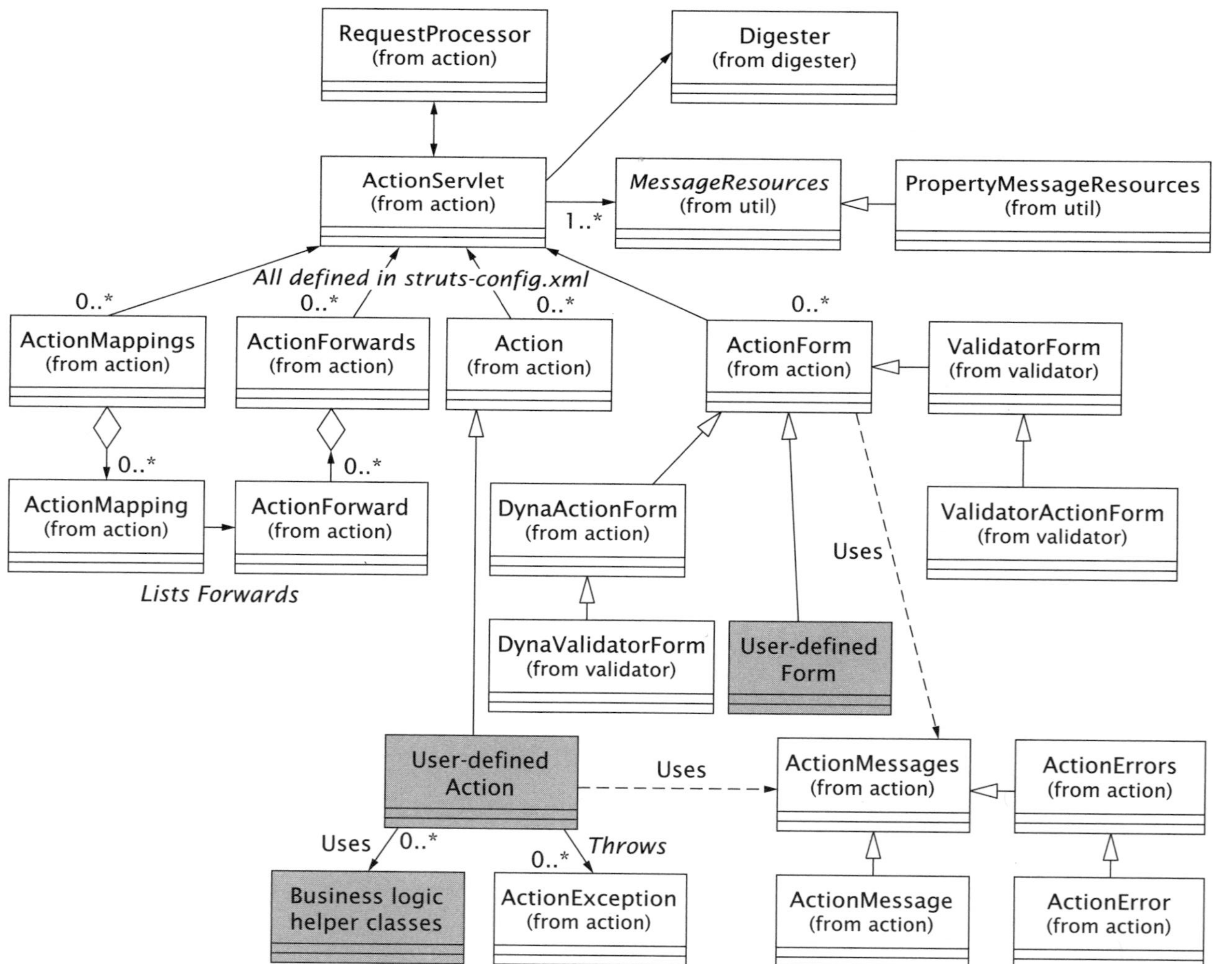


**Figure A.1:** Stuts 1.1 UML diagram.

appendix B

# Web Resources

This appendix contains all the resources listed throughout the book, organized by topic. It can be used as a quick reference guide so you can look for more information about a given subject covered in this book.

## B.1 Development Tools

*jakarta.apache.org/ant/index.html*

*jakarta.apache.org/commons*

*jakarta.apache.org/struts*

*jakarta.apache.org/tomcat/index.html*

*jakarta.apache.org/tomcat/tomcat-4.0-doc/appdev/deployment.html*

*www.mkp.com/practical/struts*

*www.mysql.com*

## B.2 Design Patterns

*java.sun.com/blueprints/enterprise/index.html*

## B.3 EJB

*java.sun.com/products/ejb/index.html*

*www.ejbnow.com*

*www.javaskyline.com*

*www.precisejava.com*

*www.theserverside.com*

## B.4 JavaBeans

*java.sun.com/products/javabeans*

## B.5 JSP/Servlets

*jakarta.apache.org/taglibs/index.html*

*java.sun.com/products/jsp/*

*java.sun.com/products/jsp/docs.html*

*java.sun.com/products/jsp/download.html*

*java.sun.com/products/jsp/taglibraries.html#jstl*

*java.sun.com/products/jsp/technical.html#syntax*

*java.sun.com/products/jsp/tutorial/TagLibrariesTOC.html*

*java.sun.com/products/servlet/index.html*

*jcp.org/aboutJava/communityprocess/first/jsr053/servlet23_PFD.pdf*

*jsptags.com*

*www.jcp.org/aboutJava/communityprocess/final/jsr053*

*www.servlets.com*

## B.6 Helpful Tools and Resources

*jakarta.apache.org/cactus/index.html*

*jakarta.apache.org/commons/collections.html*

*jakarta.apache.org/commons/logging.html*

*jakarta.apache.org/log4j/docs/index.html*

*jakarta.apache.org/struts/resources.html*

*jguru.com/faq/Struts*

*strutstestcase.sourceforge.net*

*xdoclet.sourceforge.net*

*www.husted.com/struts*

*www.jamesholmes.com/struts/console*

*www.junit.org*

## B.7 I18N

*java.sun.com/docs/books/tutorial/i18n*

*www.unicode.org*

## B.8 Logging and Testing

*jakarta.apache.org/cactus/index.html*

*jakarta.apache.org/commons/logging.html*

*jakarta.apache.org/log4j/docs/index.html*

*strutstestcase.sourceforge.net*

*www.junit.org*

## B.9 MVC

*java.sun.com/blueprints/enterprise/index.html*

*java.sun.com/blueprints/patterns/j2ee_patterns/model_view_controller*

## B.10 Sample Application

*www.mkp.com/practical/struts*

## B.11 Struts Extensions

*www.jcorporate.com*

*www.lifl.fr/˜dumoulin/tiles/index.html*

*www.livinglogic.de/Struts*

## B.12 Struts Mailing List

*jakarta.apache.org/struts/resources.html#archives*

struts-user-digest-subscribe@jakarta.apache.org

## B.13 UML

*www.rational.com/uml/gstart/index.jsp*

*www.togethersoft.com/services/practical_guides/umlonlinecourse*

## B.14 Upcoming Technologies

*java.sun.com/products/jsp/taglibraries.html#jstl*

*jcp.org/aboutJava/communityprocess/review/jsr052/index.html*

*jcp.org/jsr/detail/127.jsp*

## B.15 XML

*www.w3.org/TR/2000/REC-xml-20001006*

*www.w3schools.com/xml/default.asp*

# Index